Now Is Your Ti

"David Dean is a brilliant author!"
"His 7 Principles of selling and living will
change you from 'average' to 'leader'
once you begin following them."
Og Mandino, CPAE
Author
The Greatest Salesman In the World

"*Now Is Your Time to Win* is by a winner to anyone who
wants to excel. Buy these concepts—use them daily—and
I'll see you at the top!"
Zig Ziglar, CPAE
President
Zig Ziglar, Incorporated

"I LOVED IT!"
"And it covers all the fundamentals of good salesmanship!"
Mary Kay Ash
Founder of Mary Kay Cosmetics
Direct Selling Association Hall of Fame

"*Now Is Your Time to Win* will inspire you! David Dean's
book contains success principles you'll easily recognize,
relate to, and assimilate. If you have a definite goal and
apply these principles, you'll get into ACTION!"
W. Clement Stone
Founder
Combined Insurance Company of America

Continued...

Now Is Your Time to Win

"Read it! It works!"
"A great book to help you discover your true potential!"
David J. Schwartz, Ph.D.
Author
The Magic of Thinking Big

"This book is a tremendous winner!"
Charlie "Tremendous" Jones, CPAE
Author
Life Is Tremendous

"David Dean is, without a doubt, one of the all-time great
sales trainers and motivators in the 150-year-old history of
The Southwestern Company. His 7 Principles of
success have had a dramatic and positive impact on the
lives of thousands of people already."
Jerry Heffel
President of The Southwestern Company
Direct Selling Association Hall of Fame

"As a professional speaker and sales trainer I look back on
my life at the truly defining moments. One of the most
important was in the 1970s after an extremely disappointing
year in sales. I wanted nothing more to do with selling. My
manager David Dean persistently shared his 7 Principles
and challenged me "not to quit!" I'm glad I made the choice
to continue in sales. The very next year I tripled my production and finished number one out of 7200 sales people."
Terry L. Weaver
President
Marketing and Sales Institute, Inc.

It's not what you know
that helps you to win
—it's what you *do*
with what you know. . . .

David Dean
NOW
is your time to
WIN

**Executive
Books**

Now Is Your Time to Win

Published by
Executive Books
206 West Allen Street
Mechanicsburg, PA 17055

Copyright © 1983, 2005 by David Dean

Originally published by Tyndale House Publishers, Inc., Wheaton, Illinois

"One Day at a Time"
by Marijohn Wilkin and Kris Kristofferson.
Copyright © 1973 Buckhorn Music Publishing, Inc.,
1022A 18th Avenue South, Nashville, TN 37212
International copyright secured. All rights reserved.
Used by permission.

The excerpt from page 449 of the book, *Alcoholics Anonymous* is reprinted with permission of Alcoholics Anonymous World Services, Inc. (A.A.W.S.) Permission to reprint this excerpt does not mean that A.A.W.S. has reviewed or approved the contents of this publication, or that A.A.W.S. necessarily agrees with the views expressed herein. A.A. is a program of recovery from alcoholism only—use of this excerpt in connection with programs and activities which are patterned after A.A., but which address other problems, or in any other non A.A. context, does not imply otherwise.

Cover Design by David M. Bullock/Susquehanna Direct

ISBN: 0-937539-76-7

LCCN: 82-51199

Printed in the United States of America

Dedicated to
Dr. Barbara Lewis Dean
My wife, best friend, and partner
Thanks, Barbie.

CONTENTS

ACKNOWLEDGMENTS

With deepest gratitude I acknowledge those who have played such an integral part in *Now Is Your Time to Win*:

The Southwestern Company for sixteen great years of association and for providing such an excellent testing ground for the 7 Principles shared in my book.

Bob Wolgemuth for putting me in touch with James Hefley, Ph.D.

Dr. James Hefley for encouraging me to pursue my book project.

Susie Littleton, George Lewis, Paul Martin, and Dan Moore for their very helpful suggestions.

Rita Davenport for sharing her expertise and tips on how to conduct effective interviews.

The many people who so willingly granted the interviews used throughout the book.

Mary Kay Ash, Jerry Heffel, Charles "Tremendous" Jones, David J. Schwartz, Ph.D., W. Clement Stone, and Zig Ziglar for reviewing my book.

Og Mandino for his foreword and the inspiration I received from his friendship and writings.

Vicki T. deVries, for her expert editing and willingness to go the extra mile.

Wendell Hawley and Tyndale House for publishing *Now Is Your Time to Win*.

Charlie "T" Jones and Executive Books for the republishing of *Now Is Your Time to Win*.

Joyce Crosslin, my former secretary, for her many years of dedicated service.

Mother and Dad for their guidance and encouragement which have made such a lasting impact on my life. Special appreciation to Mother for her valuable input.

Suzie White for her help in typing the manuscript.

Barbara Lewis Dean, Psy.D. for her help on the revision of *Now Is Your Time to Win.*

Terry Ferra for her very helpful and professional assistance on the book's revision.

Marti Hefley, a truly professional writer, for her patience, persistence, and expertise which made *Now Is Your Time to Win* a reality.

FOREWORD

Reading this book will be a waste of your time.

Reading this book will be a waste of your time unless you are determined to change your life for the better, beginning right now; not tomorrow or next week or next month—NOW!

This marvelous volume, in one way, is its own worst enemy. Most books on selling, old and new alike, are dull. Reading them usually drains the most ambitious salesperson's positive mental attitude as he or she struggles throughout the usually obligatory chapters dealing with every step of the salesperson's routine from prospecting to closing. To get anything worthwhile out of most books on selling, one has to work very hard at staying awake.

Now Is Your Time to Win presents you with a different kind of challenge. Not only is its brilliant author, David Dean, one of the nation's leading sales trainers, but he also happens to be a compelling writer! That's the problem and you should be forewarned.

From the book's opening sentence, you will be swept up by the trials and travails of this gutsy man's efforts to master the art of selling. And since he tells his story in such an honest and easy-to-read style, the danger is that you will miss the thrust of his 7 Principles and lose yourself in this book as good entertainment.

So, how can you get the most from this gold mine you hold in your hand?

Read it through, the first time, for pure enjoyment. As you do, you will gradually begin to realize that you are in the presence of a very special professional who has been through every selling rejection and tribulation you have, and then some, and who has, through trial and experience, devised seven basic principles of selling and living that will change you from "average" to "leader" once you begin following them.

Percy Whiting, Dale Carnegie's managing director for so many years, once wrote, "Any fool can learn from experience. It takes a smart salesman to learn from a book—and it pays." *Now Is Your Time to Win* will pay off for you in many ways.

It will certainly increase your commissions. It will put your career in proper perspective. It will launch you toward a career in sales management, if that is your goal. Most important, it will make you proud to be a salesman or a saleswoman, one of the most difficult, and yet most rewarding, professions on this earth.

This book will change many lives. What it does with yours is up to you.

Og Mandino

TO THE READER

Now Is Your Time to Win was first published by Tyndale House Publishers in 1982. Quickly it made its way to B. Dalton's top ten bestseller list, where it remained for twelve consecutive weeks. After many years, fifteen printings and 115,000 copies sold, the book was retired.

Even though no longer available, many requests for *Now Is Your Time to Win* continued to make their way to me. It became evident that even though much of the content of the book has to do with actual events and interviews from many years ago, the 7 Principles shared are just as applicable today. After much thought, the decision was made to revise and reprint *Now Is Your Time to Win*.

The story line remains virtually the same, keeping sales and commission figures relevant to the actual years the events occurred. Wherever possible, current information regarding persons and companies that were quoted in the original manuscript was updated.

Several people that were quoted and very influential to the original book are no longer living today. I will be forever grateful for their contribution to my life and my work. They are Mary Kay Ash, Dr. James Hefley, Colonel Jim Irwin, Coach Tom Landry, Og Mandino, Colonel Harland Sanders, W. Clement Stone and Mort Utley. Their thoughts and comments were very greatly appreciated and continue to inspire.

With the advantage of an additional twenty-three years of experience since *Now Is Your Time to Win* was first released, it is my conviction that the 7 Principles outlined are totally relevant for today as well as yesterday. As you read comments from the great winners interviewed for this book, you will soon be aware that the principles apply to all professions and life in general.

The 7 Principles shared are certainly not original, nor are they profound. However, they are very basic, sound, and have stood the test of time. If you keep the principles in mind, and apply them daily, you will find yourself continuing to make progress toward your goals.

If you hit a bump in the road in your journey for success, as many of us have from time to time, go back to Principle 1 and start working the principles over again. No one desires to have a setback, but as you will read, a setback never has to be final, and with the right attitude, a lot can be learned from one. You can always bounce back if you choose.

So, let's get to it.

Let me challenge you to dig in and commit to consistently apply the 7 Principles outlined. If you do, you can be assured that NOW IS YOUR TIME TO WIN!

David Dean

1

ACCEPT YOUR SITUATION

I knew who he was and why he had come. Numbly, I handed over the car keys to the bank representative and watched him back my fully-equipped Buick Riviera out of the driveway and drive into the autumn sun. The car blended with the fall colors as it disappeared into the distance. That car had been the last symbol of my success, and now even it was gone.

I couldn't believe this was happening to me. I had been riding so high—the kid with the golden touch. At age nineteen, I had earned $7,500 selling books one summer. In 1967, that had seemed like the pot at the end of a rainbow, the good luck talisman that insured a life of continued success. Now, just two years later, I not only had been stripped of my most prized possession, but I was also $14,000 in debt.

Dazed by the reversal in my circumstances, I staggered back into my apartment as if I was in a dream. My situation seemed so unbelievably hopeless, and I felt so depressed that I began to understand how a person could turn to drink, drugs, or even commit suicide.

The idea of paying back what seemed at the time to be such an overwhelming amount was devastating. I had no job and no tuition money for my last semester. I wasn't doing well in college, my self image was punctured, and my confidence was shot. Someway, I had to graduate so I could get a decent job, but even if I managed that, it would take me years just to get even financially.

Bankruptcy went through my mind, but I just couldn't take that route since I'd talked close friends into cosigning my notes. As the days progressed, I retreated from my problem by sleeping more and more, hoping I'd wake up and find it was all a bad dream.

If I had been told at that point I could bounce back from failure to success in *thirty seconds*, I wouldn't have believed it, and I probably would have thought my intelligence was being insulted.

The summer between my junior and senior years in college, I had invested all my savings and $14,000 in borrowed money into a cosmetics company. I had been led to believe I could clear $50,000 the first year. Instead, just a few months after I joined, the company was declared illegal, and I was left holding an empty moneybag. I'd already sold my Corvette to pay my fall tuition. Yet, I returned to Taylor University in Upland, Indiana, and continued to play the part of the successful entrepreneur. However, the reality was, I was broke except for pocket money and a few dollars in a checking account.

Even after my second car had been repossessed, I kept trying to carry off the success role, but with a student body of only 1,200, that was no easy task. When friends would ask about my difficulties, I'd just smile and say, "Oh, I've just had a little setback. Nothing serious." I might have fooled some of them, but my creditors knew better.

Christmas vacation came, but I couldn't afford the plane fare to California to be with my family. Instead, I went to Kentucky and stayed with a friend who had a home care products business. I sold his assortment of cleaning products door to door, but only earned fifty dollars in commissions for the week's work. That sure wasn't going to pay the tuition for my last semester, and I was facing the necessity of dropping out of school.

My place of refuge during those dark days was the nearest Pizza King. Manager Ben Hodgin and his wife, Carolyn, demonstrated an inordinate amount of patience by letting me hang around night after night for hours at a time. The atmosphere was warm and friendly, but most importantly, Ben and Carolyn would sit and listen to my tale of woe without judging my stupidity or berating my fate. "Okay, Turkey, so you blew it," Ben would agree, "but look, you can pull out of this if you just keep your cool." Instead of sympathy, he gave me a job delivering pizzas and mopping floors.

Taylor's head football coach, Bob Davenport, former two-time All-American from UCLA, took time to counsel me. It really helped to be able to talk frankly about my situation. Except for my roommates, I was still trying to give my fellow students and professors the impression that I was still on top. With "Coach" I could be open about my situation.

"You can overcome this," Coach Davenport assured me. "And someday you'll look back at this as one of your greatest learning experiences."

I had great respect for Coach Davenport, so his strong belief that I could bounce back helped to bolster my self-image and to redirect my thinking. A short time later, a phone call came from Glenn Jackson, my former sales manager at The Southwestern Company.

"I've heard you've got a little situation," Glenn said.

"Yeah, I really have."

"Is there anything I can do to help?"

"Not unless you have $14,000 to $15,000 you don't need," I laughed.

"I heard you're considering dropping out of college."

"I don't want to, but I don't have a choice. I don't have money to repay my debt and I can't borrow more. I wouldn't want to borrow more if I could."

"How much would you need to get you through your final semester?"

"A thousand would probably do it."

"Okay, David, you'll have a check for that amount in the mail Monday morning."

"Glenn, I don't know how or when I'll be able to pay you back."

"Don't worry about that, David. Pay me when you can. Now, this is what I want you to do. First of all, quit feeling sorry for yourself. You'll pull out of this, but you need to finish college first. Right now you need to go to your creditors and assure them that you intend to pay back everything you owe, even if it is just a small amount weekly or monthly. Explain your situation to them. David, you've got to quit ignoring the problem."

"Should I sell books again next summer?"

"I don't know. That's your decision. But you and I both know it would probably be your best bet for that three month period of time."

"Glenn, I don't know how to thank you."

"Don't try."

I hung up the phone and sat there reviewing the conversation in my mind. Glenn was sending me $1,000 with no strings attached. What a vote of confidence! He had also given me some excellent advice. Now was the time to accept my situation exactly the way it was. Nursing my wounded ego, whining about my humiliation, and wallowing in self pity all these months had not helped. All the principles I had learned about being successful weren't working for me because I was not accepting my situation. I was trying to put my life back together without first laying the proper foundation. Before I could make any progress, I had to quit daydreaming that my debt would somehow miraculously disappear and start facing my problem honestly.

Honestly. That word gripped me. Honestly facing my problem would mean I would no longer have to try to pretend I was a success. It didn't mean that I had to be satisfied with the mess. I sure didn't like it, but if I had guts enough to accept it and make the commitment to do whatever was necessary to pull out of it, I could go on from there. I could quit trying to fool my friends. I could call my folks and tell them about my financial fiasco. I breathed a deep sigh. Honestly accepting my situation brought me a sense of relief. It seemed that a burden had been lifted from me, and I could feel my old enthusiasm coming back.

As objectively as I could, I considered my liabilities and my assets. There was really only one big liability: "The Debt." On the positive side, I had a family that loved me. I was in excellent health. I had friends like Ben and Carolyn, Coach Davenport, and Glenn Jackson, who still believed in me.

If I really cracked the books, I'd soon have a college degree. With 3,000 hours of sales experience gained by knocking on over 8,000 doors, I'd had a lot more experience than most of my contemporaries. I'd had a taste of success, and even though the climb out of debt looked rough and would take a long time, I was excited because I had just taken the first step.

NOW THIRTY-FIVE YEARS LATER...

As I look back on that experience, now thirty-five years later, I continue to realize just how big a step accepting my situation really was. I've also learned in the intervening years that I'm not the only one who has had to take that step. After my friend, Bill Wade, and I had finished playing a couple of sets of tennis with my brother, Doug, and a successful music personality he works with quite often, I asked the singer how he had turned his career around.

Just a few years previously, after he'd been working for seventeen years in his profession, his music group was dissolved and he was broke, thousands of dollars in debt, and perplexed about his future. As hard as it was to do, he accepted his situation, determined to return to doing those things that had worked when his career was doing better.

"I went back to the basics," he told me. That must have been the right decision. Kenny Rogers made a tremendous comeback and has become legendary in the music world.

COLONEL HARLAND SANDERS
REFUSED TO BE DEFEATED

I had the privilege of interviewing Colonel Harlan Sanders for my radio talk show, "The Winners' Circle," just a few weeks before he died at age ninety-one. He was an excellent example of a man who refused to be defeated by circumstances. When he was sixty-two years old, a new highway had wiped out his restaurant business. Colonel Sanders could have gone to Florida and spent the rest of his life in a beach chair, bewailing his bad luck. He didn't. He accepted his situation exactly the way it was. The traffic was gone. The business was dead. He took inventory of what he had left and decided he had a pretty good recipe for fixing fried chicken.

"I had a friend who had a restaurant in Salt Lake City," Colonel Sanders reminisced for me. "In the twelve years he'd been in business he'd never sold fried chicken, and I couldn't interest him in trying mine. It took some doing, but I finally convinced him to eat some. He smiled when he took his first bite and nodded at his wife. He started selling chicken like it was going out of style. He couldn't keep up with his booming business.

"That was my first franchise. After that, one franchiser would tell another what my chicken had done for him. In two years, I had 600 franchises. That highway moving away from my place was one of the best things that ever happened to me," Colonel Sanders mused. Here was a man who hadn't spent much time worrying about circumstances he couldn't control. He accepted his situation and turned the negative circumstances into one of the greatest business successes of our time.

KFC Corporation, based in Louisville, Kentucky, now has more than 11,000 restaurants in more than eighty countries and territories around the world and is the world's most popular chicken restaurant chain.

HE BRAVELY ACCEPTED HIS SITUATION, KEPT HIS COMMITMENT, AND WON OVER THE ODDS

It's only natural to feel down when circumstances seem to be going against you. However, even in the most difficult of times, if you're willing to accept your situation exactly the way it is, and commit to proven success principles, you can bounce back. One of the young men who attended the sales school held each summer at The Southwestern Company was faced with seemingly insurmountable odds. Two weeks before he arrived in Nashville, his fiancée had dropped him cold, and a week later his mother died. He came on to sales school anyway. When he picked up his commission check at the end of the summer, he ranked as one of the top out of the 3,500 first-year salespeople.

"David," he told me, "I can honestly say that half the mornings before I started knocking on doors, I was in tears. I never felt more alone in all my life, but I had made a commitment, and I felt I should keep it. And I did."

He could have spent the summer feeling sorry for himself and everyone would have understood, but instead he bravely accepted his situation, kept his commitment, and won over the odds.

MARY KAY ASH OVERCOMES CHALLENGES ON THE WAY TO BUILDING A GREAT COMPANY

Mary Kay Ash is well known because of the tremendous success of Mary Kay Cosmetics. Shortly after plans had been made to start the business, her husband died of a heart attack. She had depended on him for the administration and financial end of the business. Mary Kay could have dropped the plans for a new direct-selling business in cosmetics, and no one would have blamed her. She didn't. She accepted her situation and went on to build one of the most successful companies in the country.

Mary Kay suffered another tragic loss. Mel Ash, her second husband of fifteen years, died of lung cancer a few weeks before I interviewed her. Shortly after I entered her luxurious home in Dallas, Mary Kay was reminiscing about Mel. "He was a wonderful man who went everywhere I went," she said. "He called himself the 'father of 70,000 daughters'. When he died, I was scheduled to be in a jamboree with my salespeople four days later. I went because I had committed myself to being there, and I knew that was where Mel would have wanted me to be."

Mary Kay Ash did not allow hardship, tragedy, and numerous difficult circumstances to defeat her. In each instance she accepted her situation and became stronger as a result.

JERRY POGUE FIGHTS BACK
TO BREAK COMPANY RECORDS

In 1968, my good friend Jerry Pogue was a district sales manager with The Southwestern Company. That year he had a tragic boating accident that almost took his life. Jerry was hospitalized for two-and-a-half months, and lost the use of one arm until seven operations over many years helped his situation. Instead of allowing the accident to ruin his career, he returned to work just as soon as he could.

Jerry went from recruiting 150 salespeople the year before the accident to 200 the next year. The following year, in 1971, he recruited 417 salespeople. The year after that, he built an organization of 665 people and set a recruiting record that still stands. He went on to become Senior Vice-President of The Southwestern Company. In the nine years we worked together, I never once heard Jerry complain about his misfortune.

Jerry later went into the investment business as a stockbroker in Seattle. During his first four years and five months, he opened 14,000 new accounts, managing over $200 million in funds in precious metal stocks. After selling his business, Jerry went on to be CEO of several publicly traded Canadian mining companies. Today, he serves on the board of several successful companies. Jerry Pogue has learned to accept his situation no matter what it is and has continued to be a great winner.

COACH JOHN WOODEN WINS HIS FIRST
TWO NATIONAL TITLES UNDER VERY
CHALLENGING CONDITIONS

Over lunch one day, John Wooden, famed basketball coach and winner of ten national titles, talked with me about his early years.

"When I came to UCLA, basketball was not well thought of. Strict academic entrance standards prevented us from acquiring some of the best players. I was led to believe that UCLA's Pauley Pavilion would be completed within three years, and instead it took seventeen. I conducted practice during those years on the third floor of an old gym with the wrestlers and gymnasts practicing on the sidelines and at the other end of the floor people were working out on the trampolines. Besides these distractions, for seventeen years my managers and I had to sweep and mop the floor every day before practice, because the dust would make it dangerous for the players.

"These conditions were rather difficult, and I let them bother me for quite a while. As a matter of fact, I was at the point of developing a persecution complex. Eventually, when I accepted them, I came to realize you have to do your best with the things you can control and not spin your wheels on things you cannot control. I changed my attitude, and we went on to win the first two of our ten national championships under those same conditions."

JEANNE ROBERTSON TURNS
HER HEIGHT INTO AN ASSET

Jeanne Robertson, CSP, Certified Speaking Professional, and CPAE, is an inductee of the National Speakers Association Speaker Hall of Fame. She is an excellent example of a young lady who took stock of a circumstance she could not change and turned it into an asset. "In the seventh grade, at thirteen years of age I was 6'2" tall," she told me. "All thirteen-year-old girls seem to have problems, but this wasn't one that was going to go away. My parents were great about it, though, and helped me have a positive outlook. They helped me anticipate remarks that people were sure to make.

"Then we'd come up with a comic response. This really helped me to develop a sense of humor about my height, and I still use many of the lines we developed in my speeches. I might as well face the fact that even though I might live to be 103, I'll never be a 'little old lady.'

"One advantage I had was that I grew up in a basketball area in North Carolina. I started playing in the fifth grade and played all through high school and college. The things you cannot change, you have to accept."

The tallest woman ever to have competed in the Miss America pageant and winner of the Miss Congeniality award, she continues to be in great demand as a professional speaker. Toastmasters

International named Jeanne the recipient of its 1998 Golden Gavel Award, given annually to one individual for accomplishments in leadership and communications. Jeanne is earning top money in a demanding field because she learned to accept her situation and has used it to her advantage. She is frequently billed as "a tall gal with a tall sense of humor."

THE RICE BROTHERS "THINK BIG"

At the National Speakers Association Convention where I first met Jeanne, I also met John and Greg Rice, twin brothers who are very successful businessmen from Florida. While having dinner with them, I asked for one of their business cards. The name of their company is Think Big. "The name expresses our philosophy of life," John explained to me. "We hold motivational seminars and challenge people to think big." Naturally, I asked them how they'd gotten started doing these seminars. "First, we decided to go into the real estate business," Greg recalled, "so we took a one-week crash course, got our licenses, and started selling in West Palm Beach, Florida. Together we sold fifty-eight houses that first year, setting a record for the company we were working for. Before long we were being asked to speak to groups of realtors, and the seminars resulted."

The Rice brothers continue to be willing to accept themselves as they are. This, in spite of the fact that soon after they were born, their parents abandoned them. John and Greg Rice "Think Big" and are great men that continue to speak professionally even though each stands just 2'11½" tall.

JANET BALLAS KNOWS, "WHEN THE GOING GETS TOUGH, THE TOUGH GET GOING."

Recently I was discussing the current trends in the real estate market with my friend Janet Ballas, one of the top real estate salespersons in the metropolitan Washington, D.C. area, and for years, a true professional in the field. She told me, "The real estate business is fantastic. It continues to be challenging and ever changing, and that's okay, because so does life. This business tests you everyday and allows you to see just what you are made of. Like the saying goes, 'When the going gets tough, the tough get going,' and that's really true. I'm having some of my best months ever, but I'm 'getting to' work longer hours to do it.

"It's hard to get to the top in any profession, but it's even harder staying there. Over the years, I have learned that 'if it wasn't this challenge', it would be 'something else'. Life is never without challenges. So, it's a matter of choosing to take what could be seen as negative and counteracting it with a positive thought or action of some sort. If I worry about the client I just lost, I will lose the next two, so I don't worry about the things I can't control. I try to learn from past mistakes, but I never live in the past. I erase negative thoughts and keep charging.

"To keep making progress toward my goals, I choose to stay positive, accept each challenge as it comes, and work through each one the best I can. I'm committed to staying at the top, regardless of the challenges and difficult circumstances I am sure to encounter from time to time."

With an attitude like that, it's very obvious as to why Janet Ballas continues to be one of the very best in her profession.

MORT UTLEY SHARED, "IT ISN'T WHAT HAPPENS TO YOU THAT'S IMPORTANT...IT'S HOW YOU REACT TO WHAT HAPPENS."

When my friend, Mort Utley, was age fifty-nine, he lost his complete net worth in the real estate recession of 1974; $3 million. "I learned a lot through that experience!" he declared enthusiastically. "Believe it or not, the loss of money didn't really bother me. The fact that some people had taken advantage of me was the hard thing to accept. I did find out who my real friends were.

"Some of the men in the same company took bankruptcy as a way out and then moved away. One man told me, 'The only thing anyone could do for me is to put a .38 to the back of my head and shoot me.' Four of us just kept working, and we're all in good shape today. Those who took bankruptcy haven't recovered yet.

"It took me five years to recoup my losses. I learned that it isn't what happens to you that's important...it's how you react to what happens. If you have the right attitude, and are willing to work hard, you can always make a comeback. Happiness is in the journey—not the destination."

The following piece on acceptance is the best I've read:

ACCEPTANCE

And acceptance is the answer to all of my problems today. When I am disturbed, it is because I find some person, place, thing, or situation—some fact of my life unacceptable to me, and I can find no serenity until I accept that person, place, thing, or situation as being exactly the way it is supposed to be at this moment. Nothing, absolutely nothing, happens in God's world by mistake. Unless I accept life completely on life's terms, I cannot be happy. I need to concentrate not so much on what needs to be changed in the world as what needs to be changed in me and my attitudes.

ACCEPTING MY SITUATION FREED ME
TO COMMIT MYSELF TO BASIC SUCCESS
PRINCIPLES I KNEW WORKED

I wish I had known how to apply these principles back in my student days when I was having such a difficult time. With the advantage of hindsight I can now look back and realize some of my mistakes...

My first summer at The Southwestern Company I worked hard and finished as the number twenty-one student salesman. The next summer I recruited fifteen students from my campus and received a commission on their sales. I had the sixth best team in sales, finished number seven in the company with my personal sales, and doubled my overall profit from the previous summer.

Instead of continuing to do my best, however, I became overconfident. I didn't work as hard at recruiting during the following school year and brought only two people to sales school the next May. Additionally, I wasn't mentally prepared to start selling again.

As my third summer wore on, I became discouraged. I wasn't reaching my weekly goals. I got off schedule, and though I tried hard to get back on, I just couldn't. The last two weeks I was so psyched out that I couldn't make myself knock on a door. I was so embarrassed that I called my sales manager, Glenn Jackson, and asked him to mail my commission check to school, so I wouldn't have to face the people at The Southwestern Company. Glenn persuaded me to come through Nashville anyway. Even though I hadn't done as well as the previous summer, I had managed to finish as the number thirty salesman in the company. In the eyes of many, that was okay, but

I knew it was far below my sales goal for the summer. It's been said that the greatest burden we can carry is our unused potential, and I hadn't come close to reaching my full potential. I simply had not done my best.

A real fear swept over me as to whether or not I could make a comeback the next summer and get on a good schedule. I didn't know then that the solution to my problem would have been to accept the fact that I hadn't done as well as I had expected to and go on from there. One slow summer didn't mean I couldn't bounce back even stronger the next summer if I'd commit myself to a set of principles that would make it possible.

I had been looking for an easier way, and when I was assured that I could get rich quicker with less effort by investing in a new cosmetic company, I'd bought it. I bought it big. Then when the business went under, so did I.

After the scheme failed, I spent months feeling like a ship lost in a fog. I knew there had to be a way to return to solid ground, but all the signals were distorted. After three summers of selling, I was quite knowledgeable in motivation and success principles, but none of them could get me back on course, because I wasn't applying them. It's not what you know that helps you win—it's what you do with what you know. I could tell others how to be successful, but I couldn't break through the fog of self pity that kept me from doing it myself. I just didn't want to believe that the person who was really responsible for my problems was David Dean. I didn't want to admit to myself that I had fouled up so royally. I wanted to blame others for the shape I was in, but I knew too well I was responsible for the choices I had made.

Another reason I found it extremely difficult to be honest about my situation was that I just didn't know if I was willing to make the kind of commitment necessary to bail myself out of my problems. Finally, I recognized it was either sink or swim. I couldn't continue treading water much longer.

After the phone call from Glenn Jackson, I faced my situation squarely for the first time. I totally and completely accepted my situation exactly the way it was and decided to do something about it. That acceptance was the lifeline that put me back on course. The course was certain to be stormy, but at last the fog was gone and I could start moving.

Accepting my situation freed me to commit myself to basic success principles I knew worked. This realization, this total acceptance of my situation and the commitment to doing whatever was necessary to bounce back from failure to success, had taken only *thirty seconds*.

2

BE WILLING TO FAIL

A s I was working up courage to enter the office of the bank president, a favorite saying that I had so often repeated during my selling days came back to me:

The credit belongs to the man who is actually in the arena, whose face is marred by dust and sweat and blood; who strives valiantly; who errs and comes short time and time again; who knows the great enthusiasms, the great devotions, and spends himself in a worthy cause; who, at the best knows in the end the triumph of high achievement; and who, if he fails, at least fails while daring greatly, so that his place shall never be with those cold and timid souls who knew neither victory nor defeat.

I took a deep breath and plunged through the doorway. The broad-shouldered, efficient-looking bank executive in his pin-striped suit looked up at me quizzically from behind his massive desk.

I swallowed hard, introduced myself, and tried to sound confident as I rattled off my well rehearsed proposal of debt payment. Although he listened politely, he didn't seem too excited about the delay. He did appreciate my being honest with him about my financial situation and agreed to set up a deferred monthly payment plan. The encounter hadn't been nearly as bad as I had anticipated.

A couple of weeks later, George Butler knocked on my door. George was now a sales manager with The Southwestern Company and was doing some recruiting on campus. He talked with me about coming back to sell books the next summer. I thanked him but said, "George, I'd like to picture myself being able to do well at selling again, but I just don't know if I can. I remember when John Emery, my student manager and one of my best friends, first challenged me to sell with Southwestern. It was a hard decision, because it was straight commission with no guarantees.

"My sales experience had been limited to childhood ventures, selling personalized Christmas cards to earn my first bicycle and Mary Foelber's Butter Balls for my dad's choir fundraiser. However, I finally committed myself to going to sell books, followed John's suggestions, and had a very profitable first summer. My second summer proved to be even more successful, and I had great confidence that my third summer would be by far my best one yet. George, to my surprise, not only did I not sell as much as I had done the previous summer, the last two weeks of the summer I allowed myself to get really off schedule. It got so bad that finally I got to the place where, try as I might, I couldn't make myself knock on another door. I still don't think I've gotten over it. That was a year and a half ago. The passing of time hasn't restored my confidence toward selling. As a matter of fact, I believe the fear has become worse. George, I guess I'm just afraid to fail."

"David, I know how you feel. Everybody has fears. But failure to face a fear never solves it—procrastination only gives fear time to grow. You don't have to make a decision today. Think about it."

By the time George returned a few weeks later, I had realized there was a lot of truth to his words—the fear had grown.

"David, are you ready to make that commitment to go sell again next summer?"

"George, I really want to. You know how badly I need the money, and one of these days I need to face the fear of failure. But, I just don't know if I can produce the way I once did."

"David, maybe you can't."

"What?"

I said, "Maybe you can't, but you're never going to know until you try. There is no disgrace in failing—the disgrace is in not trying. You've got absolutely nothing to lose and a lot to gain. Look at it this way. If selling books doesn't work out, the sun is still going to shine, and you'll still have a couple of good years left to try something else. You're making this too big a deal."

He pulled out a contract and said, "Sign this thing and let's get on with it."

"George, I believe you're right. Let me think about it for a while and I'll get back to you."

"You don't need to think about it anymore. You've thought about it too much already. David, you've got to be willing to fail. Now sign this contract." Without saying another word, I took his pen and signed the dotted line. Interestingly enough, after the commitment had been made, I felt good about it. I had taken another step.

My folks gave me $200 as a graduation gift and assured me they were behind me 100 percent. I used the money to buy a '53 Chevrolet for $125. The car was nearly as old as I was, but fortunately, I was in better condition than the Chevy. I couldn't help but smile as I went driving down the highway. The car was nothing like my new Buick Riviera that had been repossessed, but it sure beat walking as I had been doing for the last few months.

Shortly after I pulled into Nashville for the start of sales school, I ran into the previous year's number one salesman, Dave Ditto. He said, "Aren't you David Dean?"

"Yes, I am."

"I've heard my older brother talk of you. You used to be pretty good, didn't you?"

"Yeah, I guess so." I decided right then that whatever Ditto's final ranking would be for the year, I was going to beat it.

At the office, I ran into Dortch Oldham, then president of The Southwestern Company.

"David, it's good to have you back with us. I hope you have a great summer. By the way, have you ever made the President's Club?"

"No, Dortch, I haven't. I've come close a couple of times, but have never hit it."

"Why not do it your first week?"

In 1970, making the President's Club meant selling $2,000 worth of books in a week. At my rate of commission, that meant a profit of over $800 for one week's work. That was quite a challenge. "Dortch, I sure will give it my best," I pledged.

The next day, George Butler introduced me to Jeff Wilson and John Reed, two crackerjack salesmen, who were to be my roommates for the summer. At the close of sales school, we all headed for Aiken, South Carolina, our sales locality.

At 7:59 a.m. Monday morning, I was headed toward my first house. The moment of truth had arrived. Despite my preparation, I was uptight wondering if I could still sell. The first lady I demonstrated books to was nice, but didn't buy. On the way to the next house I repeated, "The credit belongs to the man who is actually in the arena..."

After a few more houses, I made a sale. I was on my way. By 9:30 p.m. I had sold $480 dollars worth of books and was tired, but elated. If I could have five more consistent days, I would hit the President's Club.

Going into Saturday, I had sold $1,750. I got off to a slow start. I couldn't give a book away. I sold my first book at 3:00 p.m. At 9:00 p.m. I was still $100 short. I started looking for lighted houses. I made more demonstrations, but no sales. So close.

At 11:15 p.m. that evening I drove by a house where several couples were out on the porch talking, so I stopped. I walked up to the house and said, "You're going to have a hard time believing this but..." I sold a set of books which clinched my entry into the prestigious President's Club, and I had actually made over $800 in commissions.

At 1:00 a.m., I called Glenn Jackson to tell him the great news. At that hour of the morning he wasn't quite as enthusiastic as I was, but he was really glad to hear that I was off to a good start.

I was thrilled when the company progress report came out with my name at the top of the list. I had been willing to fail, had faced my fear, and was conquering it.

ART LINKLETTER SHARED, "I HAD A LOT OF FAILURES. BUT EACH FAILURE WAS ONLY A TEMPORARY THING."

Until that experience, I made the mistake of looking at successful people where they were, without considering what they had gone through to get there. During an interview in Phoenix, Arizona, TV legend Art Linkletter told me some of his experiences. Art had spent six years "wandering around the country" trying to break into show business. He had kept talking to film directors and broadcast executives. Finally, he got his first break on "People Are Funny" which ran every Friday on NBC for nineteen years. Then one day he interviewed his four-year-old son, Jack. He happened to have a copy of the recording with him when he called on a San Francisco station. The interview was broadcast and the mail came pouring in.

"I saw a flag waving," Art said. "Suddenly I realized how much people are interested in kids. Here was an untapped opportunity."

The result was the highly successful "House Party," which ran five days a week, fifty-two weeks a year for twenty-five years.

"Even after my first big break," Art continued, "I had a lot of failures. But each failure was only a temporary thing. You don't really fail; you just have a disappointing experience."

There's no doubt that Art Linkletter became a great winner. He won two EMMY Awards and one GRAMMY Award. He has received ten honorary doctorate degrees, and has authored twenty-three books. One of his books, *Kids Say the Darndest Things* was among the top fourteen best sellers in American publishing history and #1 for two consecutive years. His most recent book is *Old Age is Not For Sissies*. As Chairman of the Board of Linkletter Enterprises, he has been highly successful as a businessman as well. A very prolific speaker, Art Linkletter has traveled thousands of miles a year inspiring people to believe that life can be a winning experience, and that they can reach their full potential by committing themselves to persist until they succeed. All this from a man who was abandoned by his biological parents and left on the steps of a church.

MARK SPITZ SETS A GOAL FOR SEVEN GOLD MEDALS

Fear of failure keeps many people from committing themselves to attempt lofty goals and secret ambitions. Mark Spitz won two gold medals in swimming in the 1968 Olympic Games in Mexico City. Most athletes would have been thrilled to have won one gold medal, let alone two. Spitz, however, was extremely disappointed because he fell two gold medals short of his goal. It would have been so much easier for him to have retired from swimming and say, "I know I could do better in the next games if I wanted to, but I just don't want to." That would have been safe. Or he could have said, "I'm going to come back in four years and win more medals than I did last time." That, too, would have been safe. But he told the sports world that in Munich at the next Olympic Games, in 1972, he was going to win seven gold medals, a feat that had never been accomplished in the history of Olympic competition. That's what I call "being willing to fail."

Olympic champion, Bob Richards spoke to The Southwestern Company's sales managers at a meeting in Dallas. During his talk he said that when Mark Spitz told him he was going to win seven gold medals in Munich he almost laughed. Even though Richards had won gold medals in the pole vault at the '52 Olympic Games in Helsinki, Finland, and again at the '56 Olympics in Melbourne, Australia, he knew it would be almost impossible to win seven gold medals. He said he came close to replying, "Yeah, Mark, and my mother is going to run a 3:50 mile, too."

Mark endured four strenuous years of training and a lot of ridicule. Then on September 3, 1972 news from Munich, Germany flashed around the world. Mark Spitz had just made Olympic history by winning his seventh gold medal.

TOM LANDRY BELIEVED "IT WAS JUST A MATTER OF TIME."

In 1960, when Tom Landry took on the job of head coach of the newly formed Dallas Cowboys' franchise, he knew the early years would be difficult. He was right. The first season the Cowboys' scorecard read: Won 0—Lost 11—Tied 1.

It takes courage to continue to be willing to fail. Tom Landry did not have a year when his club won more games than they lost until his sixth season. "With so many defeats, what kept you believing you could produce a winning team?" I asked him, as we talked at the Cowboys' headquarters.

"Oh, I never felt we were being defeated. I never once believed it wouldn't happen. It was just a matter of time.

"Winning and losing, David, is a teaching and learning experience. You beat somebody and you're teaching him something. If you get beat, then you're learning something. You just catalog all those learning experiences until you don't make the mistakes anymore. It isn't necessarily what happens to you, but how you react, and a winner has a winning attitude even in defeat."

Coach Landry knew what he was talking about. Between 1965 and 1985, he set an NFL record: twenty consecutive winning seasons. He won thirteen NFC East titles and five overall NFC titles. With Landry as head coach, the Dallas Cowboys won Superbowl VI over Miami following the 1971 Season; and, Superbowl XII over Denver, following the 1977 Season. Tom Landry went on to become the NFL's third-winningest coach of all time compiling a 270-178-6 record in his twenty-nine years as head coach of the Cowboys. Coach Tom Landry was a great winner, on and off the field. He was inducted into the NFL Hall of Fame in 1990.

CHERYL SALEM OVERCOMES FOUR STRAIGHT YEARS OF DEFEAT TO ACHIEVE HER GOAL OF MISS AMERICA

Cheryl Salem, Miss America 1980, shared with me: "When I was five years old, we had a milkman who used to tell me that someday I was going to be Miss America. I guess that planted a seed in my mind. I entered my first pageant when I was eighteen. It was a Miss America preliminary—Miss Choctaw County in Mississippi. I lost. The next year I entered the Miss Mississippi State pageant and lost again. The following year I entered Miss Mississippi State again, and again I lost. The third year at Mississippi State, which was my fourth year in a pageant, I won the university title and thought I was finally on my way, but lost at the state level. The fifth spring I entered another local pageant and won. I then won Miss Mississippi and went on to Atlantic City and won the Miss America Pageant. But it had taken me five full years.

"The good part about winning is not winning when it is easy, but when it's difficult, when the obstacles are bigger than you can imagine, and when you've had defeats. That makes winning even greater, because you know what it's like to go through the heartbreak before you get to win!"

"WRITING MUSIC HAD BEEN BURNING HOT IN MY MIND."

Being willing to fail often means giving up security. Ron Huff started out in college to be a dentist. He switched to business, dropped out, got married, and went back and graduated. He directed choirs a few years, then took a secure job in an in-law's advertising agency. All the time he wanted to write music.

Several years after he was established in the music business, I asked Ron how he had gotten into music full time. "Writing music had been burning hot in my mind. It wasn't an easy or a quick decision, because I had been writing music for years, but my wife, Donna, and I decided this was the time in our lives when we should step out a little farther."

The Huffs moved to Nashville with three sons, no money for furniture, and no assurance of a regular income. "I gave myself ten years to reach my goals in the music business," he said. In a few years Ron

Huff became one of the top arranger/orchestrators in the country. One of his arrangements "Alleluia" has sold over a million units.

COACH BILL HODGES RECRUITS A STAR

Coach Bill Hodges was willing to fail in his recruiting efforts. One of the top high school basketball players in the nation graduated and accepted a scholarship to Indiana University at Bloomington. After a very short time there, the young athlete dropped out. He had come from a small town in southern Indiana and didn't feel comfortable at all at the big university.

Coach Bill Hodges, then the assistant basketball coach at Indiana State in Terre Haute, Indiana, became aware of the situation and decided to recruit him and bring him to Indiana State. Coach Hodges said, "He was thinking about trying out with the pros. Physically, he probably would have been able to handle the pros; emotionally, I didn't feel he was ready. He was right out of high school. To make the grade with the pros, you have to be strong emotionally. Since he'd left Indiana University, I was pretty sure he wasn't ready."

"Did you know him prior to that?" I asked Hodges.

"No. I went down to talk to him, but he really didn't want to talk to me. He'd had it with recruiters and college, and wasn't interested in returning.

"I finally found him with his grandmother at a Laundromat. He said flatly that he wasn't interested in talking with me.

"I told him I wasn't going to pressure him, just wanted to talk with him. His grandmother said, 'Oh, it won't hurt to talk.' So I went to his grandmother's house and we sat down and talked about an hour."

"What was his main objection?"

"He didn't appreciate the fact that when he'd left Indiana University, people had been really down on him."

"What changed his mind?"

"We got to talking about a friend of his who was a fine basketball player. They'd been playing AAU ball together in an industrial league. He said his friend could have made a great professional player if he'd gone to college. I told him, "One of these days they're going to be saying the same thing about you.

"I could see that really had an impact on him. I left it there, and we didn't talk anymore that day. After five days I had all the paperwork necessary. I went back and told him I had come to take him to Indiana State to college and to play ball.

"'How did you know I would come?'" he asked. "'I never once doubted it.'"

This great ballplayer went to Indiana State where he red shirted his first year because of eligibility rules. Under Bill Hodges, who became head coach, he went on to have an outstanding college career. His senior year he took Indiana State to the final game of the NCAA playoffs, and was voted the "Outstanding College Basketball Player of the Year." He was drafted by the Boston Celtics in 1979, and was the "NBA Rookie of the Year" in 1980. He proceeded to make the NBA All-Star team twelve times between 1980-1992. During those years, he led the Celtics to three NBA World Championships. You might have heard of him. His name is Larry Bird.

MARY KAY ASH PUTS HER LIFE SAVINGS INTO A COSMETICS FORMULA AND GOES FORWARD

What keeps most people from realizing their potential? Mary Kay Ash put her finger on the answer beautifully.

"Fear. Fear is the root of all of it," she told me. "Fear of rejection. Fear of not succeeding. Fear of losing whatever money you might have. All the fears that we have as human beings. If there's one equal factor where women are concerned, it's a lack of self-confidence. To see a woman so timid and shy she could hardly talk over the phone develop in a few months into a beautiful, personable woman is really wonderful.

"Mary Kay Cosmetics has grown tremendously, primarily because women are terrific. They are really able to sell, especially if it's something they believe in."

Mary Kay can speak with authority on the subject of being willing to fail. After working in direct sales for twenty five years, she decided to write a book to help other women overcome the hurdles that she had encountered. Once her ideas were on paper, she thought, *"Wouldn't it be great if somebody did this instead of just talking about it."*

"So I put my money where my mouth was and put my life savings into a cosmetic formula that I had been using the past ten years," she explained.

Mary Kay wanted to create a company that would give women an opportunity to be all they were capable of becoming. She saw beauty and ability in every woman. She believed women were capable of earning large sums of money and having the luxuries of life, including Cadillac automobiles.

With limited resources but unlimited faith, Mary Kay Cosmetics began in August of '63. From the beginning, Mary Kay was committed to keeping things in proper perspective and set out to build her company on the foundation of God first, family second, and Mary Kay Cosmetics third. It proved to be a winning formula. Mary Kay had an unwavering belief in women. She set a sterling example as a person, provided great leadership and motivation throughout the company, and produced products her sales force could be enthusiastic about.

Since '63, Mary Kay Inc. has grown from nine original sales force members to an independent sales force of nearly 1.3 million, doing business in more than thirty markets around the world. 2003 sales for Mary Kay Inc. of nearly 1.8 billion in wholesale sales worldwide certainly established Mary Kay as one of the largest direct sellers of skin care and color cosmetics in the world. Mary Kay became the second woman to ever be inducted into the very prestigious Direct Selling Association Hall of Fame. In 2003, Baylor University named Mary Kay Ash the "Greatest Female Entrepreneur in American History."

Let me ask you a few questions. What kind of goal would you set if you knew beyond a shadow of a doubt it was impossible to fail? Would your goal be a whole lot different from what it is now? What's keeping you from pulling out the stops and committing yourself to a goal that would really cause you to stretch?

ABRAHAM LINCOLN WAS WILLING TO FAIL

During my turbulent college days, I was challenged by the life of the Great Emancipator, Abraham Lincoln. I began collecting books and miscellaneous facts about him. As I learned more about him, I realized that Abraham Lincoln was a man who truly had been willing to fail.

Abraham Lincoln

1831 Failed in business
1832 Defeated for state legislature
1833 Failed in business again
1834 Elected to state legislature
1835 Sweetheart died
1836 Had nervous breakdown
1838 Defeated for speaker of state legislature
1840 Defeated for elector
1843 Defeated for Congress
1846 Elected to Congress
1848 Defeated for Congress
1855 Defeated for Senate
1856 Defeated for Vice-President
1858 Defeated for Senate
1860 Elected President of the United States

Lincoln's example and the stories of others who, by being willing to fail, had ultimately become highly successful inspired me back in those dark college days. This still didn't make my fear disappear. During the eighteen months before I went back to selling books, I had the desire to conquer the fear of failing, but I couldn't pull it off. In thinking about the lives of people I considered to be great winners, I finally realized that success is a process of setting and achieving a series of short range goals that lead to the accomplishment of a major goal.

I started reviewing my own progress. At my lowest ebb, it had been Ben and Carolyn Hodgin at the Pizza King who had kept me sane. Neither of them was a trained counselor, yet they had a great deal of common sense and were concerned listeners. Then, Bob Davenport gave me hope. College roommates Gary Rickner, Jim Messner, and Dan Gordon tolerated my moodiness and challenged me to do something about my situation. Southwestern salespeople— John Emery, Rick Turner, David T. Brown, and Mel and Judy Leach—continued to believe in me. Glenn Jackson demonstrated his confidence in me. It was encouraging to have friends who would stick with me in spite of my tough circumstances.

By associating with positive people like these, I found my outlook gradually changing. Their optimism was contagious. I realized that losers tend to gravitate toward other losers because they love to remind each other that "It can't be done." These winners helped me redirect my thinking and caused me to remember I could choose to channel my thoughts in a positive direction if I really wanted to.

After I had accepted my situation and had become willing to fail, I saw that continually rehashing the past was unproductive. I needed to control my thoughts, instead of letting my thoughts control me. *Controlling your thoughts is the ultimate discipline.*

Instead of being my own worst enemy, I befriended myself. I quit saying, "This can't be real," or "I'll never get out of this," or "Double D, how could you have been so stupid?" That was only reinforcing negative emotions. So I started telling myself, "This, too, shall pass," and "I'm going to pay back every dollar," and "Double D, look how much you're learning at a young age."

I'd smile at my reflection in the mirror and count my grey hairs, which were multiplying rapidly. I found that talking positively over and over again to myself and others really helped, because it's almost impossible to talk positively and think negatively at the same time. Repeating positive phrases reinforced my determination to win.

Getting back to reading good positive material was refreshing. I lived with Og Mandino's *The Greatest Salesman in the World.* I was helped also by *The Magic of Thinking Big* by Dr. David J. Schwartz, *Success through a Positive Mental Attitude* by W. Clement Stone, and *How I Raised Myself from Failure to Success in Selling* by Frank Bettger. I also found the Bible to be a genuine source of inspiration.

I underlined passages in these books, studied them, and even memorized passages. Finally, however, I came to the realization that it was possible to so saturate myself with information about being willing to fail that it could easily become a means of procrastination. It's easy, even enjoyable, to talk, to think, to read about being willing to fail, but to actually do it, you've got to take definite action. It took George Butler, a man who knew me and my situation, to help me make a decision on a plan of action I knew was right. I was thankful he did. People will do anything to delay putting themselves back on the line once they have failed.

That sounds as if signing that dotted line solved all my problems. If I'm going to be honest, I've got to make a confession. When I finally walked up to that first door, after eighteen months of not being able to make myself knock on a door, I was still afraid. I feared both failure and rejection. The fear didn't leave me, but I knocked on that door in spite of it.

While waiting for the homeowner to answer the door, I muttered to myself, "The credit belongs to the man who is actually in the arena, whose face is marred by dust and sweat and blood...who knows the great enthusiasms, the great devotions, and spends himself in a worthy cause...."

PRINCIPLE

3

MAKE DAILY PREPARATION

Making the President's Club that first week gave me a tremendous boost. The second week was another strong week. The third week was also good. The fourth week I hit the President's Club again, and was averaging $800 a week in commissions. I was beginning to believe that this could be my best summer ever if I could keep doing the little things that made the difference. Neglecting those "little things" had caused my downfall back in the summer of '68.

Before starting the critical summer of '70, I vowed to go back to the basics. What I learned from the mistakes of the past was that if you neglect the little things, you'll ultimately fail in the big things. Daily preparation kept me from neglecting the little things.

I began repeating the Serenity Prayer as a part of my daily mental preparation:

"God, grant me the serenity to accept the things I cannot change, the courage to change the things I can, and the wisdom to know the difference."

This prayer helped me keep in perspective what I could and could not change. I couldn't change the weather, the economy, or the attitudes of other people. I couldn't control when and who would buy. I could control my work and sleep habits. I could control my attitude and my thinking. I could control being prepared for the day. And I could control the number of calls and sales presentations I made each day.

With the assumption that daily preparation begins the evening before, I did my paperwork each night instead of waiting until morning. Before hitting the sack, I'd decide exactly where I would start knocking on doors the next day.

For me, half the battle was getting my body to a vertical position. As an incentive to jump out of bed each morning, my roommates, John Reed and Jeff Wilson, and I would nightly put money in the middle of the floor an equal distance from each bed. When the alarm went off, the first one to reach it got to keep it. There were a few midair collisions but no casualties. At 6:00 a.m. I'd be in a cold shower, singing, "It's a grand thing to be a book man..."

Then while shaving, I'd tell the man in the mirror, "This is the best day I've ever had. I can...I will...I'm going to help thirty people a day live a richer, fuller, more meaningful life because I stopped by and showed them my books. I can...I will...I'm going to, become day by day, the greatest salesman The Southwestern Company has ever had."

While dressing and getting ready, I would listen to an inspirational tape. At the diner where I ate breakfast each morning, my selection often consisted of a deluxe cheeseburger with a fried egg in the middle, French fries, and a chocolate milkshake. Admittedly, this was rather different, but I seldom took much of a lunch break, so I was kind of trying to combine the two meals into one. Over breakfast, I'd look over my sales talks and read a "scroll" from Og Mandino's *The Greatest Salesman in the World.*

Before leaving for the sales locality, I'd mentally prepare myself for anything that could happen that day. *This may be a $200 commission day; it may be a $20 commission day. A $200 day isn't going to make my summer, and a $20 day won't break it, I'd remind myself. I may make several calls where I don't even get inside. I may make several demonstrations that I don't sell. I may hit a stretch where a lot of people aren't home. Some people may be in a bad mood. It may rain. I may get another flat tire. I may have mechanical trouble. I may have some times when I don't like what I'm going through.*

By being mentally prepared for anything, I was seldom surprised. I expected the best, but was prepared for the "what ifs" and had already determined how I would handle each one. If I was selling like crazy, fine; if not, I knew it would only be temporary.

I believed in the law of averages. I had the confidence that if I would consistently work hard 12-1/2 to 13-1/2 hours a day and make thirty good demonstrations daily, then the law of averages would not fail me.

My sample case would be at the first door at 7:59 a.m. My goal would be to make at least thirty demonstrations a day. Each demonstration would take approximately twenty minutes, making thirty demonstrations in a day possible, but I had to hustle. I would aim for ten demonstrations between 8:00 a.m. and 12:30 p.m., ten between 12:30 p.m. and 5:00 p.m., and ten more between 5:00 p.m. and 9:30 p.m.

This routine would get tiresome at times, but my goal for the summer was high, and I had learned the hard way the importance of staying on schedule. *Success is not a matter of chance—it's a matter of choices.* Success isn't something you hope happens. It is high achievement accomplished by consistent daily preparation and commitment to a goal with a daily plan of action.

Accepting my situation, being willing to fail, and making daily preparation were three of the 7 Principles I used that summer to turn my life around. The *thirty seconds* in which I had faced my situation honestly and had made the commitment to do whatever needed to be done had redirected my thinking, changed my attitude, and started me back on the road to success. However, the debt still loomed over my head. Being willing to fail had meant a three month commitment to selling books, an opportunity that could start me chipping away at my monumental millstone. I felt certain that the more diligently I applied the rest of the principles, the larger the chips would be.

JOHN NABER PREPARED DAILY
TO BECOME AN OLYMPIC CHAMPION

The habit of making daily preparation is a common characteristic of many of the winners I've talked with in the years since.

Olympic champion, John Naber, shared with me how he learned this principle at an early age. In high school, he would swim daily from 5:00 a.m. to 7:30 a.m. and from 4:00 p.m. to 6:00 p.m. Every other day he spent thirty minutes lifting weights. How does a young man keep at such a schedule? "I wanted to go to the Olympics," he explained. "There are over 100,000 amateur athletes in swim training. They spend four hours a day, six days a week, eleven months a year, ten miles a day, up and down the pool.

"That doesn't sound very exciting, but we would motivate each other to keep plugging away," he stressed. "Anyone who goes to the Olympic trials has given much of his life to the sport. Only a small percentage will make the team.

"In swimming you are basically racing against the clock. I'd try to improve myself .01 or .001 of a second each time. In four years, I went from 59.5 to 55.5. I'd cut that up into amounts of .3 of a second or .12 of a second a day. I'd be racing the clock, but I'd also play mind games. I'd imagine the cheer of the crowd and the feel of the cold chain of the gold medal being slipped over my head."

That kind of consistent daily preparation was phenomenal, but John had a goal. At age twenty, he had made it to the 1976 Olympics in Montreal where the years of daily discipline finally paid off. He won four gold medals. Consistent daily preparation pays big dividends for those who make this principle a habit.

SPENCER HAYS, "AN AMERICAN ORIGINAL"

Spencer Hays, Executive Chairman of the Board of The Southwestern Company, also learned the principle of daily preparation early in life. He was raised in the small town of Gainesville, Texas, and from the age of twelve clearly remembers working hard to help support his family. Spencer became an accomplished athlete and earned a basketball scholarship to Texas Christian University. It was during his freshman year at TCU that Spencer first heard about a summer opportunity to sell books published by a company in Nashville called The Southwestern Company.

So, in the spring of 1956, Spencer borrowed forty dollars from his grandmother, Mary Moore. He and his new bride, Marlene, packed their clothes into his car, and then drove to Tennessee. Spencer spent his honeymoon learning to sell books. That was the beginning of what would be a remarkable career in direct sales. In 1960, after several successful summers of selling, recruiting, and managing, Spencer became a district sales manager with The Southwestern Company.

Over the next eleven years, Spencer built large, productive sales organizations, many years managing over five-hundred student salespeople at a time. In 1971, Spencer was given the responsibility for sales for the entire company. Two years later, Spencer Hays was named president of The Southwestern Company, the oldest and one of the most respected direct sales companies in America.

In 1992, I had the privilege of attending the awards banquet at the Annual Direct Selling Association meeting being held in San Antonio, where Spencer was inducted into the very elite and prestigious "Direct Selling Association Hall of Fame."

Now, forty eight years after picking up that first sample case, Spencer is married to his same sweetheart and serves as Executive Chairman of the Board of The Southwestern Company. Forbes magazine, Dec. 1, 1997, did a feature article on Spencer Hays entitled, "An American Original." The article acknowledged that in this true life rags-to-riches story, not only has Hays built a $400 million personal fortune, he also owns several other companies reported to have revenues of well over $600 million annually.

Spencer loves to sell. I've often heard him say, "The profession of selling is the greatest profession in the world."

Spencer believes in planning. "I really believe in priority lists. Each day I write down what my objectives are for that day and what I need to get done this week, next week, and even the next six months, and then I make sure I am working with a definite plan in mind. So many people spend 90 percent of their time on things that produce only 10 percent results. They confuse activity with results.

"That's why salespeople have so much to teach other people. A successful salesperson understands the value of organizing his day and knowing exactly where he's going to be each minute of that day. So many people have their days filled up with whatever happens to come along instead of saying, 'I've got to get these things done.'

"You have to have a plan, David. You have to be specific about the things you are going to do to reach your goal. You have to put pressure on yourself. If you are unwilling to do the things that cause you to excel and succeed today, they won't be any easier to do tomorrow or the next day. Today is the day, and now is the time."

Spencer Hays believes in utilizing spare moments during the day. "When I am on an airplane or have to wait for something, I use the time to dictate, read, or often I pull out one of the pieces of paper I always carry with me and memorize the quotes that are typed on them—ideas that reinforce my goals." Things like:

'The man who says it can't be done is often interrupted by the man doing it.'

'Consider the postage stamp—its usefulness consists primarily in its ability to stick with one thing until it gets it done.'

'There is no philosophy by which a man can do things he thinks he can't.'

"Probably few of these quotes are originals. I read them somewhere. You don't get credit for reading them. You don't get credit for underlining them. You only get the credit if you apply them. I memorize these quotes until they become a part of me.

"Sometimes emergencies may come up that take priority over everything else you had planned for the day. So you have to change your priority list for that one day, but some people use that as an excuse for never laying out a detailed schedule and plan. You see, *failures don't plan to fail—they just fail to plan.*"

"YOU HAVE TO BE ORGANIZED AND USE YOUR TIME WISELY EACH DAY...," ABIGAIL VAN BUREN SHARED.

During a recruiting trip, I boarded a plane in Spokane, Washington. Walking through the aisle, I stopped temporarily right in front of a lady bearing a close resemblance to "Dear Abby." I looked at her as if to say, "Are you?"... She took the question out of my mouth before I could utter it and said, "Yes, I am and you're welcome to join me."

During the hour flight Abigail Van Buren shared thoughts on how she managed to do a daily column for so many years: "You have to be organized and use your time wisely each day when you're constantly faced with deadlines." The stack of mail she was reading emphasized her words. Abigail Van Buren is definitely a lady who formed the habit of daily preparation. At the time she retired from writing her daily advice column, the "Dear Abby" column was one of the most widely syndicated newspaper columns in the world. With a daily readership of more than 110 million, Abigail Van Buren became one of the most, if not "the most," successful syndicated columnists of all time. In the process, being organized and daily prepared, she also found the time to write four best sellers.

MORT UTLEY CONSISTENLY
PREPARED FOR EVERY SPEECH

Mort Utley was an outstanding motivational speaker. For twenty-five years he delivered the closing speech at The Southwestern Company's sales schools. I heard that speech at least thirty times, yet each time I would find myself captivated all over again.

"How can you deliver the same speech over and over like that and still make it sound fresh?" I asked Mort.

"Preparation, David. I've given that speech probably five hundred times. I used to do it twenty times a week, yet I still listen to it on a tape a minimum of three times during the week before I give it. I also listen to it once or twice early in the morning before I go to the auditorium to speak. That way I know every word I'm going to say, when I'm going to say it, and how. It's just like a baseball pitcher warming up before a game."

THE NIGHT BEFORE AND THE MAN NEXT DOOR

One of Mort's favorite stories on the importance of daily preparation came from his forty-three years of experience in the life insurance business:

There was a man who was failing so miserably in the life insurance business that he was about to quit. His wife knew he had potential, but had watched him wake up morning after morning with no appointments lined up and no definite ideas about how to get started. Finally she said, "OK, if you're going to quit, that's fine, but at least give yourself a fair chance. Before going to bed, write down ten prospects that you would like to sell life insurance. Then call and try to get appointments with a few of them." He did and got appointments with three of the prospects. When he woke up the next morning, he was excited. He had a plan and already had lined up people he would see. One prospect he called on had just left. His partner was there, however, and suggested that as long as the man had driven that far, he might as well call on the new young businessman in the store three doors down the street. The salesman said he had a little time, so he went right down, called on the businessman and proceeded to sell the newcomer a sizeable policy. The salesman went home at the end of the day excited and feeling successful. He made a vow to himself that in the future he would do his planning the night before, and would always call on the man next door. He went on to do well in the life insurance business and called his plan "The night before and the man next door."

A man who practiced what he preached, Mort, years ago, went to a print shop and had forms printed to use in writing out his plans for the week. "I carry last week, this week, and next week with me when I travel," he explained. "That way I know where I've been, where I am, and where I'm going. I never consider a day closed until I've written down everything I'm going to do the next day. David, developing this one habit could revolutionize many careers."

This habit helped Mort accomplish a great feat within the life insurance industry. When he went with the Penn Mutual Life Insurance Company's San Francisco agency as director of training, he set a goal to make it the top producing agency in the company. At the end of twelve years, not only had he reached this goal, the agency also produced more ordinary life insurance business than any other agency in the United States.

"Forming the habit of daily preparation should be a goal of every success oriented individual," Mort stated. "Good habits unlock the door to success. Losers *let* things happen; they're merely creatures of circumstances. Winners make things happen; they're creators of circumstances."

"YOU HAVE TO HAVE GOALS," BILL RODGERS ASSURED ME.

If anyone knows the importance of daily preparation for reaching long range goals, it is the marathon runner. Bill Rodgers has run twenty-eight sub 2:15 marathons and won twenty of them. He won the Boston and the NYC Marathons four times each and held the American Marathon record for six years. In talking to Bill in August of 2004, from the Bill Rodgers Running Center in Boston, I was amazed to learn that he still holds the American track records for the 20KM, the 25KM, the 30KM, the 10 mile run, and the 1 hour run. Bill very humbly shared with me how he prepared to be able to accomplish these outstanding athletic feats.

"You have to have goals," Bill assured me. "I started running at age fifteen, back in 1963, with the Newington, Connecticut, recreation program. At the end of the summer, we had a track meet, and I ran the mile race in five minutes and twenty seconds and won the event. The following fall I joined the cross-country team as a sophomore, and I ran all through high school and college.

"I didn't enter my first marathon until I'd been running ten years. For the next ten years I averaged about 120 to 125 miles a week. You have to do that day by day—about twenty miles a day. It takes months and even years before you start running the marathons. You learn to run longer and longer distances, on a very gradual basis, month by month, and year by year. I'm always running in preparation for the next race."

Bill Rodgers, twenty-eight years after winning his first marathon, still runs sixty miles a week and competes at a very high level. He runs about twenty-five races each year around the country, continuing to inspire generations of runners. A quote at the bottom of his poster, *Relentless*, sums up Bill's philosophy on preparation and being a winner. "To be a consistent winner means preparing not just for one day, one month, or even one year, but for a lifetime." Bill Rodgers is a great winner and is definitely "King of the Roads."

"NOBODY HAD WORKED HARDER THAN I HAD, AND NOBODY WANTED TO BE MISS AMERICA MORE THAN I DID."

Consistent daily preparation pays big dividends. I asked Cheryl Salem, Miss America 1980, about the competition in Atlantic City.

"If I had gone to Atlantic City and not been prepared, it would have been a tough week. There were fifty young women there who wanted to be Miss America. But nobody had worked harder than I had, and nobody wanted to be Miss America more than I did. For six straight weeks before the pageant, I worked from 8:00 in the morning until almost midnight every day. I spent five hours a day exercising. The swimsuit contest had always been my weakest point, but I won it in Atlantic City—and I needed those points to win the title."

Cheryl continues to prepare to win in her multifaceted career. She has authored twenty books, including bestseller, *You Are Somebody*. She speaks nationally with her husband, Harry and their two sons, Harry III, and Roman. Cheryl also sings, writes songs and has recorded sixteen music CD's.

JIM MOORE REPLIED, "I FORMED THE HABIT OF PLANNING MY WORK AND WORKING MY PLAN."

I asked real estate entrepreneur Jim Moore what he considered one of the major characteristics of his steady successful climb. "David, I have formed the habit of planning my work and working my plan," he replied. "It sounds simple because it is, but it works. So few people do this on a consistent basis."

I had seen a firsthand example of that philosophy when I'd first met Jim in 1967. He had recruited a twenty man team and brought them to Nashville. I had fifteen in my team, and all of us were staying at the same motel. Glenn Jackson and other sales managers had been making a big deal about the team that managed to sit on the front row each day during sales school. On Thursday one of the sales managers said, "It's obvious Jim Moore's team is going to do well this summer—this is the fourth day in a row Jim and his men have been on the front row."

That did it. We had only one day left, so after sales school that day I called our team together, and we laid out a strategy to be on the front row on closing day. "After all, it's not how you start a race that people remember," I preached at them. "It's how you finish that counts."

We knew Jim would be going for a clean sweep on the fifth day, so we decided not to take any chances. We divided into shifts of two men each and at midnight started stationing men outside the main entrance of the small building where sales school was being held.

About 7:00 a.m., I finished my shift and went back to the room to shower. I felt tired, but proud because I knew we were about to upset the great Jim Moore team.

At 7:30 a.m., one of my men came running in shouting, "David, Jim's team is sitting on the front row!"

"What?" I exclaimed. "That's impossible! The doors aren't even open yet."

"Yeah, but at 7:30 a.m. Jim Moore and his men came charging toward us at the front door. Then, just before they reached us, they pivoted around and ran to the side entrance. Just like in a James Bond movie, a door opened out of nowhere, and a janitor let them in. Then the door was slammed shut. They waved to us through the glass doors as they walked triumphantly to the front row."

Jim told me later that they thought our team might possibly make a play for the honored seats, so he had planned ahead. He got the janitor's phone number, called him, and paid him to come in early and be at the side door right at 7:30 a.m. to pull off the caper. Even though I was upset, I couldn't help but respect the extra preparation and determination that has been so characteristic of Jim's career.

Jim started selling books in 1966. Jim was in the top twenty of all first-year salesmen his first summer and saved over $4,000. His twenty-man team from Southern Methodist University in '67 finished number one in The Southwestern Company. He then had the number one team in the company five years back to back. During Jim's last year to sell, he set records that still stand. He was the number one experienced salesman of the 958 with whom he had competed. He was also the number one student manager out of 207 managers and had managed the number one first-year salesman. He also had the number one organization in the entire Southwestern Company. His total commissions were over $50,000…which in 1967 was a "bundle."

Jim went into the real estate business in 1972. He had a couple of slow years during the recession but stuck it out. For the next several years Jim made steady progress. Then, during an eighteen-month period of time between 1979 and 1980, he sold forty-three million dollars worth of commercial property, becoming one of the very top—if not the top—real estate salesmen in Dallas, Texas.

Today, Jim is president of JHM properties in Dallas, a very successful home development and land development company that still operates in the Dallas Metroplex and the Vail Valley of Colorado.

I WAS GOING TO FIND A WAY…

It has been said, "There are two kinds of people in the world. One looks for a way and the other looks for an excuse. It doesn't take any 'guts' or 'gumption' to find an excuse—anybody can do that. It takes a quality person to find a way—to go over, around, or right straight through any obstacle that might stand in your way."

Well, I was going to be one of those people that find a way to keep making the daily preparation that was so important to staying on a winning schedule.

After I'd accepted my situation and became willing to fail, it had been the consistent daily preparation that had gotten me off to a good start during the summer of 1970. It was also a key ingredient toward producing the mental attitude that prepared me for the development of the next principle in my quest for success.

PRINCIPLE

4

BE A PROFESSIONAL

I had now been back on the book field for a month, and my sales were moving in a positive direction. I had read that the secret of success was in deliberately forming good habits. I had formed the habit of staying on a good schedule. Getting up at the same time, working 13½ hours a day, and making the calls necessary to make my daily goal in demonstrations all was paying off.

My roommates, John Reed and Jeff Wilson, were from other universities and had been total strangers to me before the summer. We had become close friends in spite of the intense competition among us. They were good schedule men—positive, highly motivated, great salesmen, and a lot of fun to be with. Jeff and John were just the right combination for me that crucial summer.

When I said the competition was intense, I wasn't exaggerating, but that was great because it kept the pressure on me to produce at maximum efficiency. Our trio was quickly becoming the top-producing "headquarters" in the whole company. At the end of the sixth week, all three of us were ranked in the top fifteen in The Southwestern Company in total production to date, with Jeff and John running slightly ahead of me. Since we had all hit the President's Club at different weeks, George Butler, our sales manager, challenged us all to hit the Club the same week. He promised to run a special write-up in the company progress report if we made it—pictures and all. That was all we needed. We were all egotistical enough to feel that was a worthwhile goal.

By Friday morning, Jeff was sitting on $1,400, and right on schedule. John had sold $1,200 and needed two $400 days to crack the $2,000 sales mark. I was sitting on $1,100 in sales and knew that somehow I was going to have to sell $900 more of books the next two days. Friday night, Jeff was up to $1,700 and was right on schedule. John had sold $400, putting him at $1,600. I knew they were both going to go over. Friday I had worked hard and given it my best shot, but had only managed to sell $200 and was sitting on $1,300.

At breakfast Saturday morning, I was rather discouraged because I felt I had let my comrades down. I knew they were getting ready to hit the President's Club, but I didn't see any way I could make it. The most I'd ever sold in one day was $550. John and Jeff had each had a $600-plus day, but none of us had approached $700. It would take a miracle for me to sell $700 on the day that would put our team into the limelight. John Reed, in his typically confident attitude, said, "Well, gosh, Dean, it's only $700. You can do that. Just go do it." I thought to myself, *"Only $700!"* Instead I replied, "Well, John, maybe you're right. I'll go for it." Because of car trouble, I got started later than usual. As I headed my '53 Chevy toward the little town of Washington, Georgia, where I was currently working, I kept thinking to myself, *"Only $700! Well, Double D, you've got nothing to lose. Let's give it a shot."* I figured I needed to sell $233.33 every 4½ hours. Even as I wrote the figure on my "crystallized goal sheet," it seemed impossible.

At 10:00 a.m., I sold a fifty dollar set. I knew that if I was going to have a chance at that $700 figure, I would have to sell sets most of the day. Single books for $32.95 just wouldn't add up fast enough.

I'd been working the area around Washington for a week and had sold books to quite a few of the leading citizens. I had some great names to use as testimonials — the mayor, one of the leading dentists, a lawyer, and the chief of police had all bought from me. Those names would have helped, but it seemed the whole town was gone to Little League Day at the local park. Few people were home. By 3:00 p.m. I had sold only $125 dollars worth of books. Selling another $575 in the next 6½ hours didn't seem very promising.

I thought, *"Maybe I'll get better results in another area,"* so I drove toward greener pastures. I don't know why, but for some reason whenever I wasn't selling well, I'd start thinking that any other sales locality would have better prospects than mine. I was about two miles outside the city limits of Washington when I thought to myself, *"David, what in the world are you doing? Here it is 3:00 p.m. Saturday afternoon, and you're getting ready to drive fifteen or twenty miles and start knocking on doors in a brand-new county with no names. You can't sell the amount of books you need to that way. At least you have good names to use in Washington, and you have a chance if you just head the car back into town and move from house to house as fast as you possibly can."*

I made a U-turn and drove right back to the house where I had left off. The family had just returned from the ballgame and proceeded to buy a sixty-dollar set of my books. I walked next door and sold another sixty dollar set. Two doors down, I sold a seventy-dollar set. At 5:00 p.m. I sold a thirty-five dollar book. I went out to the car, added up my totals so far for the day, and saw that I was right at $350. I still had $350 to go, but I had a strange feeling that somehow, someway, I was about to accomplish what just this morning had seemed almost impossible.

I'd heard the expression all my life, "When you're hot, you're hot, and when you're not, you're not." Well, I was sizzling. I moved from house to house faster than I ever had. I sold my next three customers and suddenly it seemed I was invincible. I was so excited about the possibility of hitting my goal that I felt like walking into homes and saying, "Hi, Mrs. Jones, my name is David Dean. Would you like to take a look at what you're about to buy?" I didn't really ever say that, but my bolstered confidence and positive attitude sure helped. I sold a big set of books, then went a couple doors down and sold another set, then yet another one, and at 9:15 p.m. I needed only fifty dollars to accomplish my seemingly unattainable goal. At exactly 9:45 p.m. I made the sale that put me over $700 for the day.

I walked casually back to my car, drove out of hearing distance and let out a triumphant yell. I had done it!

As I drove back toward the restaurant where Jeff, John, and I met each night, I was probably more excited and thrilled than at any point in my life. I had never shot for a daily sales goal that high. I felt as if I had just broken a four-minute-mile or had won a gold medal.

As I strolled into the restaurant, I decided to play it cool and not mention hitting my goal. I sat down and John looked right at me and said, "You did it, didn't you, Dean?"

"Did what?" I asked innocently.

"You hit $700, didn't you?"

"Yeah, I did, but how in the world did you know?" "I don't know," he said with a big smile. "I just had this strange feeling that you were going to do it."

All three of us had sold over $2,000 the same week and were in the President's Club. We celebrated over steaks, basking in the glory of our victory, anticipating that big write up in The Southwestern Company's progress report.

At the weekly sales meeting following my grand achievement, I was asked what I thought was making the big difference in my summer. After thinking about it awhile, I realized that I was looking at myself and the work that I was performing more professionally than I ever had before. In past summers, I let my emotions fluctuate too much. I had often let my feelings get the best of me and this would keep me from producing consistently. If I was excited, I would really perform, but if I wasn't excited, my production suffered dramatically. Before this summer started I made up my mind to pace myself like a trained athlete running a successful marathon, not a spirited 100 yard dash.

I shared with the other salespeople the mental gymnastics I went through each day to prepare myself mentally and emotionally. The attitude I take as I walk up to a door is if I get in—fine. If not, no big deal. If I sell, I don't get overly excited, and if I don't sell, I don't get too discouraged. I just say, 'Thank you, Mrs. Jones; I really appreciate your time. The folks next door, would they be home?' and proceed to get a little pre-approach information about the next homeowner and move.

"At the next house, if I get in, fine. If not, no big deal. If I sell, I don't get overly excited. If I don't sell, I don't get too discouraged. I just continue the routine over and over."

They didn't seem overly impressed with the secret of my success. I think some of them were looking for a "magic key." Just being consistent didn't sound exciting enough, yet that was what was working for me. Maintaining a consistent professional attitude became a principle that I applied throughout the summer. I was beginning to realize that professionals pace themselves and develop the habit of performing regardless of how they feel.

That was one of the greatest lessons I learned while selling books. I didn't always feel "healthy, happy, and terrific" or feel like knocking on doors, but I found that if I would discipline myself to get started each morning at the right time, the battle was half won.

SELLING IS "MOTIVATING SOMEONE TO ACT POSITIVELY ON AN IDEA OR PRODUCT YOU PRESENT."

Over the years, I've come to realize just how valuable that sales training has been to me. Most people are involved in some kind of selling situation every day. Selling is "motivating someone to act positively on an idea or product you present." When you are trying to motivate a group of sales people, or just making a presentation to your company; when a teacher presents an idea to his or her class; when a doctor tries to explain to a reluctant patient why surgery is necessary; when a mother is teaching a principle of good behavior to her child; when a lawyer is presenting a case to a jury; when a coach is motivating a group of players; when an engineer is justifying a new project; when a candidate for an elected office is making a campaign speech—all of these situations involve selling.

Studies have shown that only 15% of an individual's overall success will be directly related to the technical knowledge of his or her field. The other 85% will be directly related to the ability to work with and through people to accomplish specific goals. The skill of communicating well to sell specific ideas is vitally important.

I asked "Dear Abby" what she considered to be one of the biggest problems in our country today, and without hesitation she replied, "Communication. If people could just talk out what's really on their minds, a lot of the problems could be solved long before they pass the point of no return."

TOM McDOW BELIEVED IT WAS POSSIBLE

The Southwestern Company in Nashville receives letters almost daily from successful alumni of the program, people who are excelling in virtually every profession. Many of these winners attribute a great deal of their success to the principles and training they received while selling for The Southwestern Company.

Tom McDow is a great example. He set a goal of building one of the top fund-raising companies in America. As president of Great American Opportunities, Inc., based in Nashville, Tennessee, Tom started out with thirteen sales representatives and did 800,000 dollars' worth of business the first year.

During the next seven years, the company averaged a remarkable compounded growth rate of 55 percent a year.

I asked Tom why he felt the company was able to grow at such a rate.

"I believed it was possible," Tom told me. "To recruit a sales organization in the beginning, I had to sell the idea that it was possible. We had no statistics to impress anyone and no sales record, so I had to sell belief. I'm sure thankful for my sales training, because even as president, I constantly have to sell ideas on a daily basis."

"You also must have needed to accept your situation in the fact that you were starting a brand new company with no past sales figures to use in recruiting."

"I sure did," he laughed. "Someone suggested that I fake it until I make it. That's pretty much what I did at first."

"Did you have a fear of failure?"

"I certainly did. Fear of failure isn't all bad, though. It kept me working intensely."

"What about daily planning?"

"As the company grew, I saw an even greater need for planning. I had to take time to think, plan ahead, and look at the overall perspective. Each Sunday night I made a list of the things I wanted to accomplish in the coming week. Then I ranked them in order of priority."

"From your experience, what do you think defines a real professional?" I asked.

"That's tough to put your finger on. I do know that a lot of people don't really know what they want out of life. They just drift along. If we know what we really want, we can channel our energies toward reaching that goal. A professional knows what he wants and is willing to discipline himself to make the choices and the sacrifices necessary to accomplish his goal. It's impossible to achieve a goal unless you have a definite picture of it in your mind. Only then can you work to make that image a reality."

"What are some practical principles that you have found helpful?" I continued.

"Every day each of us is faced with many decisions. Several times a day I ask myself, *Is what I'm doing right now the single most important thing I should be doing in relation to my goals?* Because I know that if I can make decisions on what I should do—even if at times I don't like it—then in the long run when I've accomplished the goals I've set, I'll be glad I did.

"People who have really excelled are extremely result-oriented and have formed the habit of making decisions on the basis of pleasing results, not just pleasing activities. It's not what you do or how much you do. It's what you get done that counts."

Tom McDow continued sharing. He said, "One of the greatest thrills and joys in life is that of achieving and accomplishing worthwhile goals. It's like the great Vince Lombardi said, 'I believe that man's greatest hour, in fact, his greatest fulfillment, is that moment when he has worked his heart out and for a good cause lies exhausted but victorious on the field of battle—whenever, wherever that field of battle may be—in your business, in my business, or wherever.' "

Over the years, Tom McDow's professional philosophy and leadership has continued to be highly effective. In a recent conversation with Tom in September of 2004, I learned that Great American Opportunities, Inc., one of the most successful companies of its kind, now has 250 fundraising consultants serving the forty-eight contiguous states and has raised over $600 million for schools and non-profit organizations since 1975.

JIM McKEACHERN BELIEVED TOM JAMES COULD BECOME A $100 MILLION DOLLAR COMPANY

Jim McEachern is another man who learned the principles of success while he was working as a book man. Jim McEachern became president of one of America's finest clothiers—Tom James Company. Tom James has a group of professionals that sell tailor made clothing to executives in the convenience of their homes or offices. It was a rather new concept when Tom James was founded in 1966. "The company's total sales the first year were approximately $190,000" Jim stated. "As one of the company's first salesmen, I started talking about Tom James becoming a $100 million company as far back as 1967. Many people were skeptical that it could ever happen," Jim went on to share.

"After becoming president of Tom James in January, 1973, I clung to that vision, made a commitment to the $100 million goal, continued to prepare, and took action. I knew it would take awhile, so we set a short range goal of doubling our production every two years. By 1982, the company was doing $30 million in sales, and was right on schedule for that $100 million." In 1992, Tom James crossed the $100 million dollar milestone. In 1996, the company hit the $200 million a year sales mark.

When Jim stepped down from his position of CEO and President of Tom James, the company was doing $248 million a year and had become the world's largest manufacturer and retailer of custom clothing. When I talked to Jim, who is still heavily involved in leadership development for the company, in July of 2004, he told me, "Tom James is having its best year ever in sales and profits."

"WE SET A GOAL TO HAVE THE CITY'S LARGEST DENTAL PRACTICE."

Dentists, Dr. Mike Buehler and Dr. Mark Gravbrot, sold books for six summers and built large sales organizations before graduating from dental school. They decided to set up a practice in Yakima, Washington, even though there were already fifty dentists in the town of 50,000 people. "We set a goal to have the city's largest dental practice," they said. "It was a big goal, but we had a plan of action. We called on every single dentist and sold ourselves well enough to get referrals from most of them. At the end of two years, we had the second largest practice in Yakima, and at the end of six years, the largest. We started with two chairs and one assistant, and by 1982, we had ten chairs and fifteen assistants and were on schedule to do a million dollars' worth of dental work."

Today, Dr. Buehler and Dr. Gravbrot have individual practices. While recently talking with Mike, I wasn't surprised to learn that combined, their practices have twenty-eight chairs, and fifty employees. In 2003, they did over $5,000,000 dollars worth of dental work. In 2002, Dr. Mike Buehler was awarded the prestigious, "Citizen Dentist of the Year" for the state of Washington, presented to him by the Washington State Dental Association.

These former book men were able to fulfill their dreams because they were well trained and very professional in their work. They set specific goals, believed their goals could be accomplished, and worked hard consistently for many years to achieve them.

COLONEL JIM IRWIN SET A GOAL TO WALK ON THE MOON

One of the most inspiring interviews I have ever conducted was with a man who was able to see his childhood dream fulfilled. In July, 1971, Apollo 15 Astronaut, Colonel Jim Irwin, walked on the moon.

"My mother used to tell me, 'Son, that's foolishness. Don't waste your time thinking about it.' " Colonel Irwin, author of *To Rule the Night*, recalled. "I joined the Air Force and became a test pilot to qualify for the astronaut program. It took many years and many disappointments, but my third formal application was accepted.

"So you knew what you wanted to accomplish with your life and you worked toward that goal?" I asked him.

"Yes, but that was only the beginning. After I was accepted into the program by NASA in April, 1966, I spent another year in formal training. Lots of classroom work. Then I was assigned to the lunar module, and spent more time working with the factory that produced the vehicle. And I did a lot of testing.

"I had to develop new flying skills at the Navy's helicopter school in Pensacola, Florida, because the lunar module is a hovercraft.

"Next, I was trained as a geologist. I had to be a pretty good field observer so I would feel at home when we got to the moon. It took about five more years of training.

"It was hard work, but I would get caught up in the enthusiasm. My single goal was somehow to reach the moon. To fly in space! We all felt this was the most important thing we could do with our lives, and we were willing to give our lives if that was required. We realized there was some risk, a chance we might not come back. But we had faith in ourselves, in the hardware, and in the people we were working with. The closer it came to the flight itself, the more I prayed.

"After lift-off, as we saw the earth getting smaller and smaller, we came to appreciate it more. We were gone for twelve days, July 26 to August 7, 1971. When we reached the moon, we decided we could do our best job on the surface if we were well rested. So after landing, we opened the top hatch, took some pictures, then climbed back in and bedded down for the night. We were pretty excited when we first landed, but we tried to approach this in a very calm and relaxed manner.

"The next morning as I squeezed out in my space suit, I tripped and stumbled. I thought, *'Here the whole world is watching Jim Irwin make his grand entrance—and I'm going to land on my backside!'* I reached out and grabbed a rung of the ladder and sailed out of the view of the television camera, and in so doing my attention was drawn directly overhead—and there was Earth! Just the size of a little blue marble. I said, 'Lord, I'm on the moon! I've made it.'

"It had taken almost a lifetime of preparation—twenty years. For twenty years I'd been preparing for that moment, and it was worth every bit of the effort."

Colonel Jim Irwin accomplished his goal, because he had a plan and a commitment to that plan.

LORETTA LYNN WORKED HARD
WITH A PLAN AND A STRATEGY THAT
HAS GIVEN DIRECTION TO HER CAREER

This principle of the importance of being a professional was reiterated to me by country music "Hall of Fame" member, Loretta Lynn. Her life story is a rags-to-riches tale known by just about everyone. *The Coal Miner's Daughter*—referring to a hit single, an album, a best-selling autobiography, an Oscar-winning film, and to Loretta Lynn—has journeyed from the poverty of the Kentucky hills to Nashville superstardom to her current status as an honest to goodness American icon.

While talking with Loretta, I asked her why she felt she had been able to accomplish all she had in the music business. She smiled and without hesitation said, "Hard work! I've worked extremely hard, and I am still doing that. I've only taken one day off since Christmas. I also had a plan and a strategy that has given direction to my career." Loretta Lynn didn't become a professional by reaching the top; she reached the top because she had a professional approach toward her career from the beginning and was committed to years of hard work to accomplish her goals.

COACH LANDRY WAS COMMITTED TO BUILDING
THE DALLAS COWBOY'S INTO WORLD CHAMPIONS

Tom Landry stated, "During football season I work seventeen hours a day, seven days a week." No one made him do that. He decided long ago he was going to excel as a professional football coach. That doesn't mean you have to work seventeen hours a day to be successful. It does mean if you are going to excel there is a price to pay. There are no short cuts to the top.

DEAN JONES FELT HIS FUTURE
WAS IN ACTING SO HE "STUCK WITH IT."

One evening, I was talking to Hollywood actor Dean Jones and his wife, Lory, in their San Fernando Valley home. Dean mentioned the 100,000 hopefuls in Hollywood, trying to make it as actors. "There is more to it than most people think," he assured me. "You don't just blow into Tinsel town and get your name in lights. My first job was at Knotts' Berry Farm where I did four shows a day for thirty dollars a week. Later I was able to join MGM and had a few minor parts. I tried Broadway where I worked with a well known actress in her first play. I thought the play was my big break, but it ran only three weeks.

"After that, I wasn't able to find any work for an entire year, and I got pretty hungry, sometimes literally, but I felt my future was in acting, so I just stuck with it." Dean didn't quit. He persisted and went on to star in a successful weekly TV show, and ten Walt Disney movies, including *Love Bug*, which had one of the ten highest box office draws in its decade.

There's a lot to be said for people who hang in there month after month, year after year, as they continue to learn the skills of the trade. More times than not, people who are at the top of their professions had paid their dues to get there and to stay there.

ZIG ZIGLAR SPEAKS HIS WAY "TO THE TOP"

When I think of a true professional, motivational speaker Zig Ziglar quickly comes to mind. Zig is a CPAE and an inductee in the National Speakers Association Speaker Hall of Fame. Since 1970, Zig has traveled over five million miles across the world delivering life improving messages. He has written twenty-three books on personal growth, leadership, sales, faith, family and success, including bestseller, *SEE YOU AT THE TOP*. His books and tapes have been translated in thirty-seven different languages.

While jogging with Zig at a National Speakers Association meeting in Phoenix, Arizona, he mentioned that running was a very important part of his day. "I'm an avid jogger. Keeping in shape physically helps me stay alert mentally. I do some of my most creative thinking while running."

"Zig, how did you earn the credentials to merit $5,000 a speech?" I asked.

"David, I was starving to death as a salesman. A speaker named P. C. Merrell persuaded me that I could do things with my life I had never before dreamed possible. I went on to do well in sales and management, and then I decided I wanted to be a motivational speaker.

"I made literally thousands of speeches in my own mind, before I ever spoke from a platform. Then I spoke at every opportunity—to garden clubs, Lions, Rotaries, any place, any time I could get two or three people who would hear me. Sometimes I wondered if it was ever going to happen, but it was worth every bit of effort and sacrifice.

"It took ten years and three thousand speeches before I got my first check for a speech." Ten years and three thousand speeches. That persistence and professionalism is why you continue to see Zig Ziglar "At the Top."

HARMON KILLEBREW BELIEVES "THE ONE WHO EXCELS... MANAGES TO GET BACK UP ONE MORE TIME."

At a sports banquet in Yakima, Washington, I had the privilege of talking to Harmon Killebrew, a member of the "Baseball Hall of Fame." His 573 career home runs rank fifth on the all-time list and second only to Babe Ruth among American League sluggers. Killebrew said he believed one of the greatest professionals he personally had ever known was a man by the name of Lou Brissi. He went on to share the story.

Brissi had just started his baseball career at age nineteen when World War II broke out. He was drafted. During a beach assault in Sicily, he was hit in the leg by enemy shrapnel. Overhearing the medics discussing amputation, he begged them to try to save the limb. "I'm a professional baseball pitcher. If you take my leg, my career is over."

Fifty-six operations later Lou reported to the Philadelphia Athletics. Manager Connie Mack said sympathetically, "Lou, I don't know if you can make the team, but we'll give you a chance." Lou took his wind-up a little differently, but he could still get the ball over the plate. He made the team.

"His first time out he pitched against the Boston Red Sox. After he'd struck out the first two batters, Ted Williams came to the plate. Brissi got two strikes on him before Ted smashed a line drive up the middle.

"That was one of the hardest hit balls I'd ever seen!" Killebrew recalled. "The ball struck Lou on his bad leg, knocking him off his feet. A hush fell over the crowd. Connie Mack came running out to the mound."

Lou looked up and pleaded, "Mr. Mack, don't take me out. Please. As much as this hurts, it doesn't compare with what I've been through. Let me finish what I've started."

"Okay, go ahead, Lou," the old skipper said. Painfully, Lou picked himself up and went on to win nineteen games for Philadelphia that year. Killebrew concluded his story with the comment: "Lou Brissi epitomizes what it takes to be successful in sports or business or life. I've never known a truly successful person who wasn't knocked off his feet a time or two. The one who excels is the one who, no matter how many times he's knocked down manages to get back up one more time."

"IT IS TRUE, THERE IS NO GAIN WITHOUT PAIN."

Ann Kiemel Anderson, writer, speaker, and author of twelve books, including *I'm Running to Win,* shared with me that preparing to run her first marathon was one of the hardest things she has ever done: "David, it taught me that to be faithful to a sport or athletic event, to be faithful to God, to physical health, or to anything, there's a price that has to be paid. And it is true that there is no gain without pain."

"IT'S REALLY HARD TO GET YOURSELF MENTALLY UP FOR EVERY MATCH...," SHARED STAN SMITH

I had the privilege of serving as captain of my college tennis team at Taylor University.

We had the good fortune of winning four consecutive HCC (Hoosier College Conference) championships, and went 30-0 during those years in conference play. The competition wasn't "Big Ten" caliber of play; but, it was great to compete, and very satisfying to win nevertheless. Our big claim to fame was that my senior year we beat Purdue 7-2.

During my tennis days, I had long been an admirer of pro tennis player, Stan Smith. He beat Ille Nastase in a hard fought, five-set match to win the 1972 Wimbledon men's singles title. Stan Smith also represented our country extremely well, playing on each of the winning United States Davis Cup Team's between 1968-1972. While having breakfast with Stan at Hilton Head Island, I asked him what the most difficult part was about playing the professional tennis tour.

"It's really hard to get yourself mentally up for every match," he explained. "It's especially challenging when you switch time zones and have spent all night on an airplane, traveling to get to another country to play a new tournament."

Stan Smith is a true professional and performs regardless of how he feels. In every field, one of the biggest differences between top producers and those who never reach their potential is that the top producers perform consistently regardless of feelings.

"SINCE I HAD ALREADY GIVEN MY WORD TO UCLA, I DIDN'T WANT TO BREAK IT," SAID COACH JOHN WOODEN.

Professionals stick to commitments. It may be hard to do at times, but if an individual will form the habit of sticking to commitments, it guarantees to pay long term dividends.

Coach John Wooden, one of the greatest men that I have ever had the opportunity to meet and interview, is someone who believes in keeping his commitments. This came out very clearly as he was sharing with me how he was recruited to UCLA to be the head basketball coach.

"My second year as head coach at Indiana State we were runner-up for the National Championship at Kansas City. I received job offers from larger universities. UCLA put in a bid. But since I played college ball for Purdue, I wanted to stay in the Big Ten. I had pretty well decided to take the position offered at the University of Minnesota. The athletic director was to obtain final approval from the board, and he was to call me at a specific time. The call didn't come. UCLA phoned, again offering me the head coaching position. I accepted it. An hour later the call came from Minnesota."

"So, Coach, is it safe to assume that if the University of Minnesota had called you one hour earlier, you would have gone there instead?" I asked.

"That's correct. If it hadn't been for a late April snowstorm that prevented the athletic director from getting to a phone, the call would have come on time. Since I had already given my word to UCLA, I didn't want to break it."

This gave me tremendous insight into the character of the man who, while head basketball coach at UCLA, won an unprecedented "Ten NCAA Championships." We all know records are made to be broken, but I believe it is safe to say, Coach Wooden's record of ten NCAA championships will hold for many years to come...maybe forever.

LARRY BIRD WAS ALWAYS TRYING TO IMPROVE

Another characteristic of a real professional is that he is teachable. In talking to Coach Bill Hodges about Larry Bird, I learned that Larry developed a highly professional attitude long before turning pro. "Larry never questioned anything I told him to do," Coach Bill Hodges told me. "Larry's greatest characteristic was not necessarily his physical ability. It was his ability to make all his teammates relish playing with him. He was so unselfish. He was very humble and always willing to give the whole team credit for success. To him, success was something to be shared with his teammates. He had phenomenal court awareness. He knew what was going to happen five seconds ahead—a blink of an eye before it happened. He had great concentration. Larry was not as good a shooter in the pros as he was in college. He injured his finger. He messed it up bad, and he couldn't control the ball as well with that hand as he used to. However, he learned to compensate for that. He was always trying to improve. He never got to the point where he thought he knew it all."

MY MENTOR

Professionals realize that success is not a matter of chance, but of choices. A professional chooses to do whatever is necessary to reach his goal, whether he feels like it or not. He is willing to put forth that extra effort that the amateur considers too much trouble, too time consuming, or beneath his dignity. The pro is always learning, improving his skills, refining his expertise.

While attending a National Speakers Association meeting in New Orleans, I walked into a session on "How to Structure a Speech."

Glancing around the room, I noticed an empty chair next to a friend of mine and his wife. I walked over, we exchanged smiles, and I sat down. While listening to the lecture, I wrote down a few of the speaker's ideas. Then I realized the man sitting beside me was taking many more notes than I was. I found this very interesting, because not only was my friend a professional speaker himself, but I happened to know he earned about three times as much per speech as the man leading the session.

That really impressed me. Here was this craftsman concentrating so intently, trying to pick up a few new pointers, working continually to polish his already polished performance. I had to conclude that his willingness to keep learning must be a big part of the reason he has over thirty-nine million books in print, considered to be the best selling self help author in the world, and continued to be in such high demand as a speaker. The friend and mentor I'm referring to was none other than that master storyteller himself, Og Mandino.

IN THE SUMMER OF 1970, I BEGAN TO DEVELOP A FEW OF THESE PROFESSIONAL CHARACTERISTICS

Being teachable to that degree is another quality that marks a real professional. Back in the summer of 1970, I began to develop a few of these professional characteristics. It's a good thing too, because after that great day when I sold $700 worth of books that enabled me to join my friends in the President's Club, I was in for a real letdown.

5

LIVE IN THE PRESENT

Coming off my $700 day, I was really pumped. Monday, I got off to a good start and Tuesday and Wednesday were highly productive days as well. By Thursday morning, I had $1,000 in sales and was right on schedule for another great week. I was feeling good, even though by 11:00 a.m. the day was already a scorcher, and I was off to somewhat of a slow start.

Did I say *slow?* That was an understatement. I hadn't sold anything, but I was certain I was going to. Whenever I felt myself beginning to get discouraged, I'd read a couple of the motivational reminders I had written on cardstock and taped to the metal dashboard of my faded green '53 Chevy. "Smile!" "Relax!" "Be enthusiastic!" the cards would remind me, and I'd stride confidently up to the next door. No sale.

"Okay, David, don't let it get to you," I'd tell myself. "You have a lot of good names of people in the area you have sold, and you are building a good prospect list for this evening. It isn't really all that hot... just a normal warm summer day. Quit trying to figure out how you can last until 9:30 tonight. Just concentrate on making it 'til noon."

See that next house? I'd ask myself.

Yeah.

Can you go knock on that door?

Yeah.

Well, go knock on it then.

I'd give my sales talk, but no sale. Then I'd tell myself, *See, I didn't sell there either.*

Wait a minute, we're not going to talk about that last house. That last house is history. See that next house?

Yeah.

Can you go knock on that door?

Well, yeah, I guess I can knock on one more door.

Well, go do it. We'll talk about it later.

No sale.

See that next house?...

I'd keep playing these games with myself, trying to keep myself going, repeating positive slogans to keep me motivated. The hotter it got, the more tired I got of saying, "This is the best day I've ever had. I can, I will, I'm going to..." But I did it anyway because I knew it would help me keep a positive attitude.

As I drove to the house, I checked out the dashboard again and noticed the picture I had taped of Babe Ruth smiling at me. The line under his picture was a reminder to me. "He just kept swinging." The Babe had been a real professional. When he'd get into a hitting slump, he'd refuse to change his position at the plate, the way he held his bat, or his magnificent swing. He knew he was good, and also knew that if he'd just be patient and keep swinging, he would soon start connecting again. I was going to connect too! Confidently, I tucked my shirttail into my slacks and marched up to the next house.

No sale.

Determinedly, I reminded myself, *"That house is history. Forget it and go on to the next."* I climbed back into my Chevy and looked around for another encouraging word. "Remember Herman Osgood." That one always made me smile, because of course, no one remembered Herman Osgood—he quit! Well, I wasn't going to be a quitter! I approached the next front door, smiling optimistically.

No sale. My footsteps were dragging a bit as I returned to the car. This was getting to be a bit much. I wasn't even getting to make many demonstrations, and I was running out of signs on my dashboard. I wasn't ever going to pay off my debts at this rate. With no job lined up for the future and all my time devoted to door-to-door selling, I knew I had to a have a very successful summer. "Whoa, wait a minute, David," I commanded. "You're letting yourself slide down into self-pity, which won't help you one bit! *The hardest thing to do is to live in the present. It's unrealistic to live in the future and it's impossible to live in the past. The farthest thing away is a second ago. So settle down and concentrate on the task before you. Now is all the time you have, so make the most of it."*

I knew logically that made a lot of sense, but all that good advice was hard to follow with the sun beating down on me and my scorecard reading zero. I stopped at a little country store and bought an ice cold Pepsi. Sipping it slowly, I thought, *"Living in the present and concentrating on the task at hand seems obvious enough, but it's very hard to keep from thinking negative thoughts and worrying about the future when things aren't going well.*

"It's impossible to think a negative thought and a positive thought at the same time," my mind shot back at me.

"That's true," I admitted. "If I can just make myself think positive thoughts, then it becomes impossible for the negative ones to grab hold. I'll control my thinking. Controlling my thoughts is the ultimate discipline. *And I'll do it!"*

In that thirty-second conversation with myself, I had *solidified* another winning principle. Living in the present was the only logical way to tackle a difficult problem. I had learned from my past mistakes, and there was nothing else to be gained from continuing to dwell on the past. I could think about some long range goals during my leisure hours, but the present was all I could control. Whether I felt like it or not, my present task was to knock on another door. So I finished my Pepsi and headed for another door.

A pleasant faced lady answered and let me know she wasn't interested in buying anything from a door-to-door salesman. Her determination seemed to match my own. As I was continuing my conversation, she proceeded to close the door. I'd had only a few doors slammed in my face during my career…but a number of people had closed doors slowly while I was still talking.

As I was walking down the steps, I thought, *"That lady really did seem very nice. I'll bet she has a good sense of humor."* On impulse, I dashed around the house to the back door and knocked. When she opened the door, she seemed a bit shocked to find me standing there smiling.

"What in the world do you want?" she gasped.

"Ma'am, I hope you are a whole lot friendlier than the lady I met at the front door," I replied with a smile.

I believe she wanted to get mad, but she was so startled she actually started laughing.

"Well, at least that's different," she admitted and then said, "Oh, come on in." I gave her an enthusiastic demonstration, and she bought a couple of books.

That sale, I felt certain, had turned my day around. Now there would be no stopping me.

But it didn't work. To my great chagrin, the rest of the day it seemed I couldn't give a book away. When I pulled into our regular restaurant that night, I had a grand total of $40 in sales. My commissions totaled about $16, quite a decrease from my $700 day when my commissions were close to $300. Although a little disappointing, I was determined not to get discouraged. *"Today is over, David. Just chalk it up to experience,"* I told myself. So I did.

The next morning I rolled out of bed and repeated, "This Is the Beginning of a New Day" by Heartsill Wilson that Mort Utley had shared with us in sales school.

This is the beginning of a new day. God has given me this day to use as I will. I can waste it or use it for good. What I do today is important because I'm exchanging a day of my life for it. When tomorrow comes, this day will be gone forever, leaving in its place something that I have traded for it. I want it to be gain, not loss; good, not evil; success, not failure. In order that I shall not regret the price I paid for it, may I have sufficient wisdom and courage that this shall be my record for today?

After breakfast I returned to the same sales locality and sold over $400. The days all averaged out, and I ended up with about $1,800 in sales for the week. It came about because I'd stuck to the principle I'd been learning, the one about living in the present.

Each day I tried to concentrate on making that day a success. I'd tell myself, *If you can have a successful day, you can have a successful week, summer, year, career. I don't know if I can work this hard the rest of my life, but I can work hard today. Now is my time to win.*

MARIJOHN WILKIN WRITES
"ONE DAY AT A TIME."

Marijohn Wilkin wrote the famous song that expresses this same sentiment. *One Day at a Time* is probably the best known of the one hundred plus songs this member of the Nashville Songwriters' Hall of Fame has written. *One Day at a Time* was recipient of the BMI One Million Performance Award, and has been recorded by over 200 different artists. When I interviewed Marijohn in her lovely suburban home, I asked her what had inspired her to write this very well known song.

"It wasn't inspiration as much as a total need for help," she replied in her usual frank manner. "It was about eight years ago, and it had been a bad year. My mother had just died. My marriage was on the rocks. My business partner had left me, and I had never been in publishing alone. It seemed like the old domino theory just one thing after another.

"So I just sat down at the piano, and I sang that whole chorus just as if it were written on the piano. I just sang it, and I knew it was a great song. I wrote it down as fast as I could. Then I jumped up and called Kris Kristofferson, who had worked for me before he became famous. "Man, I've written a hit," I told him.

"The chorus I just sang out, and the second verse came really easy, but being a professional writer who works at my craft, I knew the verse I had was not the way the song was supposed to start. Kris came over and helped me put together the first verse."

"Has the philosophy of the song helped you in your own life?" I asked.

"Oh, yes! I still try to live that way," she stated. "There's just so much you can do in a day, and you are in trouble if you start worrying about what's coming. You cannot live in the past. If you have had a bad hurt in your life, that's sad, but that goes with living. I feel sorry for people who constantly live either in the past or on a promise of the future. What's the matter with right now? Right now is the time to live life to its fullest."

The words of her song, *One Day at a Time*, express her philosophy beautifully:

> *One day at a time, sweet Jesus,*
> *That's all I'm asking from you.*
> *Just give me the strength to do every day*
> *What I have to do.*
> *Yesterday's gone, sweet Jesus,*
> *And tomorrow may never be mine.*
> *Lord, help me today, show me the way*
> *One day at a time.*

J. FRED LANDERS WAS COMMITTED TO STAYING AND BUILDING A GREAT SALES ORGANIZATION

When a successful individual has business reversals because of circumstances beyond his control, that's the time to live in the present. J. Fred Landers, former Executive Vice-President and Vice-

Chairman of The Southwestern Company, had this experience. He started in the book business as a student in 1935. He was making progress building a strong sales organization until he was called into the service in World War II.

"When I got out," he said, "the student managers I had worked with before being called into the service were scattered everywhere. I had only four left. These four student managers recruited 16 students between them, and I recruited 15 students for my personal team. That gave us a total of 31 salespeople. The next year I brought 75 to sales school. In '48 the number was 155 students. Then in '49 I grew my organization to 313 salespeople."

Those were 100% increases...three years in a row. Not only is that impressive, but it is the only time in the history of The Southwestern Company that a sales manager has ever done it.

"But then the Korean War came in 1950, and I dropped to 175," he continued. "A lot of my student managers were going into the service. It was hard to recruit new students because they were being drafted right and left.

"The key to growth is the student managers, and I didn't have a lot of control over getting them back. I found it's a lot harder to build an organization than to maintain it. It took me until 1954 to grow back to 300 students.

"But I had a system, and I knew it worked, and I kept on working it. I knew from experience that I could rebuild. I had grown to over 400 salespeople when the Vietnam War started, and I was faced with the same problem all over again."

"How did you learn to live in the present in situations you couldn't control?" I asked him.

"Well, first I was committed to the business. I never gave serious thought to giving up. I was determined to stay and build a great sales organization. I knew this was what I wanted to do. The minute someone in a profession starts vacillating between staying or leaving, he doesn't put as much effort into it. I knew I'd just have to rebuild all over again.

"I went on to become part-owner of Southwestern and we built the company from a sales force of 800 to over 4,600 in less than ten years."

I had the privilege of knowing J. Fred Landers for many years, and I know he never allowed situations he couldn't control to keep him from living in the present. He formed the habit of concentrating on the task he had before him, and this enabled him to succeed in spite of difficulties that would have made a weaker man give up. Landers Plaza in Nashville, Tennessee, the home office of The Southwestern Company, is a tribute to the lasting and very positive impact he had on the lives of so many, mine included.

COACH BEAR BRYANT FOCUSED
ON THE GAME AT HAND

I had the privilege of talking to the legendary Coach Bear Bryant a few days after Alabama beat Penn State, enabling him to tie Alonzo Stagg's 314 game wins record. I asked him, "What's going through your mind being just one game short of becoming the coach with more wins than any other coach in the history of football?"

"The only thing I'm thinking about is how to beat Auburn University—and in an intellectual way at that. All this other whoopla stuff going on around us I try not to think about too much."

This was a man who knew how to live in the present. Instead of basking in the glory of past accomplishments or of the honors certain to come his way in the future, he was concentrating on the major task at hand. Mental discipline had a lot to do with the phenomenal success that Coach Bear Bryant achieved. The following week, November of '81, history was made when Alabama beat Auburn 28-17. While Bryant's 323 major-college victories have been eclipsed by Penn State's Joe Paterno and Florida State's Bobby Bowden, Bryant left a legacy that encompassed more than 37 winning seasons overall and five Associated Press national championships at Alabama.

"CONCENTRATION," COACH LANDRY ASSURED
ME, "IS ONE OF THE MOST IMPORTANT HABITS
ANYONE CAN DEVELOP."

Coach Tom Landry talked about the importance of concentration. "Concentration," Coach Landry assured me, "is one of the most important habits anyone can develop. Once you allow other things to come into your mind and break your concentration, you can't function the same.

"Some people say I'm not emotional. What I'm doing is concentrating on what's happening," he explained. "I can't cheer the great play that just happened. I have to be thinking about what the opposition may do next. If I show emotion, I break my concentration. I keep my eyes on the game. If I even look at the scoreboard, I've broken my concentration."

BILL WADE REALIZED "I'VE GOT TO GET MY MIND OFF MYSELF AND CONCENTRATE ON WHAT I'M DOING RIGHT NOW."

Athletes can teach us all a lot about living in the present. My friend, Bill Wade, quarterbacked the Chicago Bears to a national championship in '63, scoring both touchdowns on the way to defeating the NY Giants 14-10 at Wrigley Field. While traveling with him to a speaking engagement, I asked him, "What's the greatest challenge in professional football?"

After a little hesitation, he replied, "Concentration." Bill shared an experience that took place on an extremely hot day in training camp in Rennselaer, Indiana. "The sun was beating down and I wasn't looking forward to eight hours of practice. My mind was on myself, David. When your mind is on yourself, nothing tends to go quite as well as it should. We had a big game coming up in just two weeks. I was feeling a lot of pressure. How was I going to do in the first game? Would my arm be in good shape?

"I was also thinking of the people who were watching us practice, the coaches, and the other players. A lot of attention was on me as the quarterback. All these things were bothering me. Finally, I just told myself, *'Hey, I've got to block this stuff out. I've got to get my mind off myself and concentrate on what I'm doing right now.'*

"So I did. I took the ball, cocked my arm, and fired right into the chest area of the receiver who was warming up with me. He threw the ball back, and again I faded back and fired, heading in a second time right on target. I just kept throwing the ball back and concentrating on hitting the target.

"Then an interesting thing happened. As I was concentrating totally on what I was doing, I forgot the heat. I forgot about the eight hours of practice. I forgot about the people watching. I even forgot about the big game coming up. I really began enjoying just throwing the ball."

CHARLIE "TREMENDOUS" JONES
LIVES IN THE PRESENT

A winning principle in football, selling, or anything else in life is living in the present and concentrating on the immediate challenge. When you are living in the present, your mind zeros in on what you have to do right now. One of the greatest advocates of this principle is motivational speaker, Charlie "Tremendous" Jones. Charlie entered the insurance business at age twenty-two with one of America's top ten companies. By age thirty-nine, his organization exceeded $100,000,000 of insurance in force.

At that same time, Charlie founded Life Management Services to share his experiences through seminars and consulting services. Now, with over 10,000 speeches and seminars under his belt, Charlie Jones, CPAE, is a highly respected inductee of the National Speakers Association Speaker Hall of Fame. Charlie is author of the bestseller, *Life Is Tremendous—7 Laws of Leadership*, which has more than 2,000,000 copies in print. As President of Executivebooks.com, Charlie is probably the greatest promoter in the country I know of for the reading of good books. I have often heard Charlie say, *"You are the same today as you will be five years from now except for two things, the books you read and the people you meet."*

In a conversation with my long time friend one afternoon, I said, "Charlie, talk to me about living in the present." This is what he replied.

"You live in the present, because the future takes care of itself. The past is done. You live in the present when you learn there is nothing else but the present," Charlie declared. "That doesn't mean you don't plan. It means you don't spend *all* your time dreaming. Dreaming is great—if you're doing it in bed! But now is the time to *work!*"

"Charlie, what keeps a lot of people from living in the present?" I asked.

"They get so bogged down in what they did yesterday—and so scared to death about what is going to happen tomorrow—that they just can't get anything done today," he replied. "It cripples them. I'm an authority on the subject, because I am the worst offender. At least I'm ahead of most people, because I realize I'm an offender. Once you realize what you're doing wrong, you can do something about it.

"If I find myself getting concerned about tomorrow or feeling bad about yesterday, my subconscious *says, 'Pal, you'd better get to doing what you gotta do, or you are just compounding your problem.'* That's what self-motivation is all about—training your subconscious. You develop this the same way you develop any habit. You start with the simplest habit, and then you build the next one. You don't worry about the big ones until you settle the simple ones. After learning that, you can capitalize on what you've got to do—whether you like it or not. That's what determines your future."

Knowing that living in the present is important, Charlie is able to do so by keeping his mind centered on his goals and a definite plan of action. By doing this, he can eliminate negative thoughts that could keep him from performing at top capacity. Living in the present allows Charlie Jones to maintain a positive attitude, even in the midst of some serious health challenges. Forming the habit of living in the present can have a very significant and positive impact on every career.

"THE OPTIMIST AND THE PESSIMIST"

An optimistic outlook on life is a great asset, and it can help you live in the present. Mort Utley's story about the young optimist and the young pessimist certainly illustrates the point. He told it for thirty-six years, sharing it yearly in sales school. It goes like this:

There were parents who had six-year-old twin boys, who were extreme opposites. One of them was the world's greatest optimist; he loved everybody and everything. The other one was the world's best pessimist; he hated everybody and everything. The parents were so disturbed by the extreme opposite characteristics in these two boys that they took them to a psychiatrist. They said, "You've got to help us. We just don't know what to do."

The psychiatrist declared, "I can't imagine two boys in the same family, especially twins, being such extreme opposites. But I have a test for boys like this."

So, the parents and the doctor took the little extreme pessimist down to a room that had every kind of toy a child could imagine. The psychiatrist said, "Sonny, all of these are yours. You have a good time, and we'll come back after a while." They went out and shut the door.

Then they took the little extreme optimist down to a room that didn't have one thing in it except a great big pile of horse manure right in the middle of the floor. The psychiatrist said, "Sonny, have a good time, and we'll come back after a while."

In about twenty minutes, the parents and the doctor went to the room where the little pessimist was. He was seated in the middle of the floor with his arms folded. He hadn't touched a single toy.

The psychiatrist asked, "Sonny, why didn't you ride on that rocking horse?"

"I was afraid I'd fall off and break my arm." "Well, why didn't you skate on the roller skates? That would have been fun."

"I was afraid I'd fall down and skin my knees."

"Well, why didn't you blow up those balloons? Those balloons get real big, and they've got pictures on them."

"I was afraid I'd hurt my mouth."

"Why didn't you eat some of that candy? That's good candy. All the kids like that candy."

"I was afraid I'd get a stomachache."

The psychiatrist turned to the parents and admitted, "He's in pretty bad shape. But let's go see what the other boy is doing."

They returned to the second room. When they opened the door, the kid was bent down over the horse manure, slinging it just as hard as he could. He had it all over the ceiling, all over the walls, all over the floor, all over himself.

The psychiatrist took one look and said, "Sonny, what in the world are you doing?"

The little boy looked up at him and grinned. "With all this manure, there's got to be a pony in here somewhere!"

In sales school, after the laughter died down, Mort continued: "I'm going to let you in on a little secret. Don't tell anybody. But this summer you're going to have to wade through an awful lot of it. But just remember, the more there is, the bigger the ponies."

"TAKING IT ONE DAY AT A TIME IS SO CENTRAL TO THE RECOVERY PROGRAM IN A.A."

While working on this chapter, I decided to include one rather lengthy quote, because it has been a great help in keeping me focused on the present. I had no idea who had written the short essay titled "Just For Today," but I knew it was widely distributed by Alcoholics Anonymous, so I put in a call to their offices in New York City.

A gentleman named Robert P. told me, "Taking it one day at a time is so central to the recovery program in A.A. that the principle has been passed on from one sponsor to another since the founding of the organization. It has always been one of the most important parts of the A.A. program of recovery."

"Robert, what would you say to a person in recovery to get them through a single day?" I asked him.

"I would ask, 'Do you think you could stay away from a drink for one day?' And he might answer, 'I don't know.' "

I would then ask, "What about an hour?"

"If he said he wasn't sure about getting through an hour," I would ask, "All right; if that's too long, what about five minutes?"

If he agreed he felt pretty certain he could make it five minutes, I would say, "Good. In five minutes let's talk again."

"So you would actually walk people through a day?" I asked.

"Yes, we do it all the time. In my own case, I encountered this idea after my first A.A. meeting. Incidentally, my sponsor was a citizen in high standing, drove a Porsche, had a black belt in karate, and had an obvious zest for life. He also had about thirteen years of sobriety."

"At the end of the meeting, he asked what I thought of it," and I said, "Not much. How can you be so cheerful when you know you're never going to have another drink the rest of your life?"

"He said, Oh, I haven't quit drinking for the rest of my life." Of course, my ears perked up immediately at that."

"Oh, no?" I responded."

"No. I could drink tomorrow," he said. "In fact, considering my life history, some people would think it quite likely that I might drink tomorrow, but I haven't had a drink today. It's 9:00 p.m. and I believe I can make it to midnight. When tomorrow morning comes, I'll get down on my knees and ask God to help me stay away from a drink for that day too.

"Then it began to dawn on me that this was the way one does it. You don't have to quit for the rest of your life. Only quit for today. It's incredible! All I did was quit for today, and before I knew it, I had twenty-five years of sobriety," the gentleman shared.

Robert informed me that A.A. didn't have a copyright on the essay I wanted to use, and assured me it would be fine to reprint it. Then after I hung up, I got to thinking about what he had said, and the more I thought about it, the clearer it seemed that this principle could be applied to most of the problems we face. Living in the present sounds so simple, yet it is often something we fail to make a habit of doing. To do so we have to quit reliving past mistakes and not spend time worrying about the future. Reading the following each morning can help develop the habit of living in the present:

JUST FOR TODAY

JUST FOR TODAY I will try to live through this day only, and not tackle my whole life problem at once. I can do something for twelve hours that would appall me if I felt that I had to keep it up for a lifetime.

JUST FOR TODAY I will be happy. This assumes to be true what Abraham Lincoln said, "Most folks are as happy as they make up their minds to be."

JUST FOR TODAY I will adjust myself to what is, and not try to adjust everything to my own desires. I will take my "luck" as it comes, and fit myself to it.

JUST FOR TODAY I will try to strengthen my mind. I will study. I will learn something useful. I will not be a mental loafer. I will read something that requires effort, thought, and concentration.

JUST FOR TODAY I will exercise my soul in three ways: I will do somebody a good turn, and not get found out; if anybody knows of it, it will not count. I will do at least two things I don't want to do—just for exercise. I will not show anyone that my feelings are hurt; they may be hurt, but today I will not show it.

JUST FOR TODAY I will be agreeable. I will look as well as I can, dress becomingly, talk low, act courteously, criticize not one bit, not find fault with anything, and not try to improve or regulate anybody except myself.

JUST FOR TODAY I will have a program. I may not follow it exactly, but I will have it. I will save myself from two pests: hurry and indecision.

JUST FOR TODAY I will have a quiet half hour all by myself, and relax. During this half hour, sometime, I will try to get a better perspective on my life.

JUST FOR TODAY I will be unafraid. Especially I will not be afraid to enjoy what is beautiful, and to believe that as I give to the world, so the world will give to me.

6

DO YOUR BEST

T he long, hot summer days quickly turned into weeks, and I found myself in the home stretch and running well. Then I opened the envelope containing The Southwestern Company's top contender list—the total ranking of the top salespeople to date. I was elated to discover I was number six on the list.

News like that just had to be shared, so I put in a call to California. "I've got great news, dad!" I exploded. "I just found out I'm number six out of the 700 salespeople."

"That's great news. We're really proud of the progress you're making this summer."

"Now I'm faced with a new challenge."

"What's that, David?"

"I just realized for the first time that I have a real shot at being number one. But there's also the reality that I could pull out all the stops, go for it, and still not finish at the top?"

"Well, let's put it this way, if you don't do your best, you won't get it done. If you do your best, it sounds to me like you believe you've got a good chance of finishing number one. But, if you do your best and still don't finish at the number one spot, you're still a winner. How's that? David, there is nothing better than the self satis-faction that comes from knowing you have done your best. Doing your best is more important than being number one. When you know you have done your best, you win self respect.

"You've done well this summer, David, and your mother and I couldn't be more proud of you. It sounds to me as if you really want to aim for that number one spot, so, go for it! Give it all you've got. Someone is going to be number one. It might as well be you. Just remember you can't control what your competitors are doing. You can control yourself and your own performance. So, just do your best!"

"It's really kind of amazing to think I'm even in contention, but you're right. All I can do is my best. Win or lose, I'm going to try. I'm going to do everything I can to be number one, but if I don't make it, it won't be because I didn't do my best."

"David, just remember, we love you, and we'll be pulling for you."

"Thanks, Dad, that means a lot."

After I'd hung up, I thought about just how much it did mean to know my folks had confidence in me. Having a dependable source of encouragement is a tremendous asset.

My father was also a great example of a man who had formed the habit of doing his best. As the head of the music department at different universities, he was a great recruiter of talented singers and musicians. He'd also taken on the responsibility as choir director at a number of churches and, often starting from scratch, he would consistently build fantastic choirs. Dad was a real professional and seemed to have a gift for bringing out the best in people, which is one of the reasons he became one of the best music directors in the country.

Thinking about my folks made me realize there is more to having a rich life than just accumulating a lot of money. My parents always had a life rich in friends, in music, in accomplishment, and in the knowledge that they have inspired many others along the way. They taught me that real success is not measured in just dollars and cents. *Real success is the personal satisfaction that comes from knowing that you have done your best to reach your fullest potential in what you have chosen to do.*

With this attitude, I began my campaign for the coveted spot at the top. I was feeling good about my chances of making it when a call came from George Butler in Nashville. "David, we are in the process of hiring a district sales manager for next year, and I've been sharing with Spencer Hays how well you've been doing this summer. He wants you to take the next flight to Nashville to talk about coming with Southwestern Company on a professional basis."

For once in my life, I was speechless. I had looked at the sales managers in The Southwestern Company as men on white horses! To me, they were the epitome of success in business. They had not only had a good financial opportunity, but also the opportunity to influence young people in a very positive way.

"David, are you still there?"

"Huh, oh, yeah, George, I'm here. What should I wear…and what about the rest of the summer?"

"Spencer won't care what you wear," he laughed. "You'll still have time to get back on the book field and finish out the summer. I'll look forward to seeing you at the airport."

On the flight to Nashville, I contemplated meeting Spencer Hays…The Spencer Hays. He held several records with The Southwestern Company, and in my mind was a real pro. The more I thought about actually talking with him, the more nervous I became. Not even the new grey pinstriped suit I had just bought for the occasion could overcome the feeling of inadequacy that was welling up inside me.

"Now, wait a minute, David," I reprimanded myself. "You're not maintaining a professional attitude. You keep up this negative thinking and you're going to blow the interview. Aren't you always saying that the best sales talk in the world is the truth? OK, so now you're going to try to sell yourself. Just apply the same principle. Be yourself. Relax. Do your best."

George Butler and his wife, Harriet, met me at the airport and whisked me off to the plush St. Clair's Restaurant, where we were greeted by the very distinguished Spencer Hays. His dark eyes sparkled under his thick eyebrows, and the rest of his face was lighted by a big smile. "Hi, there! My name is Spencer Hays," he said while extending his hand. "I've heard so many good things about you that it is an honor and a privilege to be standing in the presence of one of the greatest salesmen in the company."

I was a little embarrassed by the flattery, but enjoyed it just the same. We ordered our meals and proceeded to have a very pleasant conversation. Spencer asked me a bit about my background, but very little reference was made to my being a sales manager. After about an hour of casual conversation, he paused, looked me in the eye, and asked, "David, can you recruit?"

I swallowed hard, and hesitated for what seemed like about *thirty seconds* while I quickly reviewed the 7 Principles I had developed during the summer. They had helped me have a successful summer, and the firm conviction developed in me that those same principles could help me become a successful sales manager.

"Yes, sir," I replied with newly found confidence. "I can."

Spencer looked at me thoughtfully for a moment and then with no comment in response to my reply, said, "Meet me in my office tomorrow at 10:00 a.m., and we'll talk more about it."

The next morning, after a very extensive interview, I flew back to the book field with instructions to call Spencer in three days. During that waiting period, I found it harder than ever to concentrate on the task at hand. My mind kept gravitating to the question, "Do I or don't I have the much desired position?" Wednesday about noon I placed the call.

"Spencer, this is David Dean."

"Hi, David! I've been expecting you to call. A lot of thought has been given to this decision, and I'm happy to inform you that I am looking forward to working with you in the capacity of a District Sales Manager. We're proud to have you with The Southwestern Company."

When I hung up the phone, I let out a sigh of utter contentment. I had the job. Dad was right—doing my best did pay. I still didn't know if I was going to finish number one, but I was already a winner. I'd won a coveted position as a District Sales Manager with one of the most established and respected direct sales firms in the nation.

OLYMPIC CHAMPION TRACY CAULKINS
FORMED THE HABIT OF DOING HER BEST

Tracy Caulkins formed the habit of doing her best at a young age. She started swimming competitively at age eight. In Berlin in 1978, at age fifteen, she became the first woman ever to win five gold medals and a silver at a world championship. At age sixteen, Tracy became the youngest recipient ever selected for the Sullivan Award, given annually to the nation's top athlete. By the time she was nineteen she held fifteen American records, and was inducted into the International Swimming Hall of Fame as an Honor Swimmer.

I talked with Tracy a few days after she broke Johnny Weissmuller's fifty-year-old record to become winner of more national championships than any swimmer in American history.

"How much time do you spend in the water?" I asked her.

"I train four-and-a-half to five hours a day, six days a week. I've been doing that for the last five years."

"How do you keep yourself motivated to work that hard, Tracy?"

"Well, you look at the goals you have for yourself and for your team, and you know you aren't going to reach those goals unless you train hard. Working toward a goal makes you keep at it. All along I've just tried to do the best I could, and all these titles have just sort of happened."

"So you consider all your success a result of the habit of doing your best?"

"Right. To do my best I've got to work as hard as I can at practices. Then, when I swim a race or compete, I concentrate on doing my best. The workouts give me confidence that I will be able to do my best. My main priority is to win, but if I get second or third place and I know I did the best I could, that's okay. If I lose and I know I could have done something better, that's frustrating."

"What did you feel like when you were about to swim the race that would break Weissmuller's record?"

"I wasn't thinking about the all-time record, actually. I was just trying to concentrate on that one race, trying to win and do the best I could. After I'd won it, I felt honored. I guess it's quite an accomplishment, but I really don't think it's going to hit me for a while."

"Do you have any advice for young swimmers?" was my final question.

"Well, just to continue to train and have fun. And don't worry if you don't seem to be improving, because it will come if you keep concentrating and working hard. Success will come if you continue to do your best."

Tracy continued to do her best and continued to win. As a student at the University of Florida, she went on to win twelve NCAA national championships, and was twice an academic All-American.

In the 1984 Olympic Games in Los Angeles, as the captain of the U.S. Swim Team, she set an Olympic record in the 200-meter medley and also won gold medals in the 400-meter event as a member of the 4 by 100-meter medley relay team. She retired after the Los Angeles Games, having won forty-eight national titles, and set sixty-one American and five world records in her career. She is a member of the Halls of Fame for Tennessee Sports, Women's Sports, International Swimming, and the U.S. Olympics. I think it is safe to say, Tracy Caulkins did her best.

Today, Tracy Caulkins Stockwell is one of the owners of Tracy Caulkins Physiotherapy Centers. Beginning in Nashville, Tennessee in 1996, over the last eight years TCPC has steadily expanded to thirteen outpatient physical therapy centers in Tennessee.

JOHN NABER'S FOCUS WAS SWIMMING HIS BEST

The importance of doing your best was illustrated by another great swimmer, John Naber. He told me that his goal in the 100 meter backstroke in the 1976 Olympics in Montreal had not been to win a medal, but to swim the distance in 55.5 seconds. "I told myself, if I went 55.5 and someone else went 55.3, there would be no reason for disappointment," John shared with me. "I would still be a success, because I would hit my goal on the money and I'd have done my best."

The record book shows that he won the 100 meter backstroke in 55.49. He beat his goal by one hundredth of a second. If someone else had won it, John wouldn't have been bitter. Either way he would have won. In the same Olympic Games, John went on to win three more Gold Medals, one silver and broke four world records, becoming America's most decorated athlete at those games. During his career he won twenty-five National AAU titles and set a record by winning ten NCAA individual titles. He led his team to four undefeated seasons and in 1977 won the James E. Sullivan Award as our Nation's Outstanding Amateur Athlete.

Today, John Naber, author of "Awaken the Olympian Within," is an effective motivational speaker, and is a television analyst, commentator and host for ABC Sports. He is also a successful businessman as the president of Naber and Associates, Inc., a consulting firm that specializes in sports related marketing. John believes, "Olympic champions are not extraordinary people. They are ordinary people who have accomplished extraordinary things in the area of their lives that matters most."

JIM CALDER KNEW "IF JUST ONE OTHER MAN IN THE COMPANY WAS HIGHLY SUCCESSFUL, THEN IT WAS POSSIBLE TO DO IT."

One of the most difficult things to face is the possibility of doing your best and working as hard as you can while your efforts seem to go unrewarded. This is especially true if you have gotten off schedule and are finding it difficult to get back to doing whatever is necessary to succeed. Then it is time to return to Principle 1—Accept Your Situation—exactly as it is, and start reworking the 7 Principles.

Jim Calder found himself in this situation shortly after he became

88

a district sales manager with The Southwestern Company. Sales managers are rated primarily on their ability to increase business, and Jim's first year he worked harder than he ever had in his life to do just that. Yet he only increased 6.8%. His second year he redoubled his efforts and saw a 16% increase. Other sales managers were seeing increases of 40%, 60%, and 100% in a single year. Jim hung in there and kept plugging away. In his third year, his business increased only 4.4%.

Jim continued to do his best. In his fourth year, all his persistence and dedication paid off. He grew 86%, earning more in that year than he had in his first three years together. The next two years he set several recruiting and production records that still stand. I asked him how he managed to keep doing his best during those discouraging years when he wasn't producing well.

"I had a few good cries," he confided. "I was broken up inside because I didn't reach my goals. I did a lot of rationalizing. I got mad at my boss because I felt he had talked me into a job that was ridiculously difficult, if not impossible. Then I got mad at myself, because others were succeeding where I was failing. Finally, I came to understand one fundamental truth. The problem was me. Because I knew if there was one other man in the company who was highly successful, then it was possible to do it. The responsibility, therefore, was not with management or the company or the territory, but with me.

"With that in mind I asked myself, *Do you really want to accomplish something with your life? If you really, really do, then you are not in a battle with the business. You are in a battle over whether you will ever be anything or not.* I had a choice of going into other businesses, but I felt that the results would probably be the same until I, Jim Calder, became the kind of individual who could rise to the occasion under any circumstances. I decided I couldn't win by quitting.

"I'm convinced that all of us have to win this battle with self if we really want to accomplish something with our lives. The battlefield might not be the book field; it can be an athletic arena or some other discipline, but you've got to win this war with self. Only then can you truly do your best in whatever you attempt."

Jim Calder went on to become one of the all time great sales managers and leaders at the Southwestern Company. He is also considered one of the finest speakers and sales trainers Southwestern ever had. Today, Jim Calder is a Certified Senior Advisor and runs a very successful financial planning business in Dacula, Georgia.

COACH JOHN WOODEN ..."MY DEFINITION OF SUCCESS IS THE SELF SATISFACTION OF KNOWING YOU HAVE DONE THE BEST YOU ARE CAPABLE OF DOING."

Coach John Wooden also had some interesting things to say about doing your best. "No player at UCLA ever heard me mention winning. I was constantly talking to the team about doing the best they were capable of doing, to try to make the most of their own potential. I'd remind them that they could have no bearing on what others can do, but they could have control of themselves.

"I believe that if you do your best, the scores will be more to your liking. Before every game I would say, 'When the game is over, let's be able to hold our heads high—and the score will have nothing to do with that.'

"My definition of success is the self satisfaction of knowing you have done the best you are capable of doing."

It's evident that Coach Wooden has applied that same philosophy to his private life, for he has twice been selected California's "Father of the Year."

DAVID T. WYATT HAD A GREAT ATTITUDE, WAS CHEERFUL, AND TOOK PRIDE IN HIS WORK

Not all winners become household names. For years, my travels through the Atlanta Airport were brightened by conversations with David T. Wyatt, who had the valet service in the men's room. David always had a great attitude, was cheerful, and took pride in his work. Although he had a limited education, he accepted his situation and worked hard to accomplish his goal of putting his three daughters through college.

"I worked twelve hours a day, seven days a week," David, who is now semi-retired, told me. "I had my bad moments, but most people appreciated me. Lots of them would compliment me, and I got to know many of them.

"My daughters? Oh, they are all fine," he announced with evident pride. "One is a high school teacher, another teaches in elementary school, and the third is in civil service."

In my eyes, David T. Wyatt is a successful man. He's done his best with what he has and has maintained a great attitude while doing it.

"I CANNOT BE SOMEONE ELSE, SO I JUST TRY TO BE THE BEST CHERYL I CAN BE."

Cheryl Salem, the lovely young woman who, after five years of trying, finally became Miss America 1980. She has also had to learn to overcome physical difficulties. "When I was eleven, I was in an accident," she confided to me. "My left leg was crushed, my back was cracked, and I had over 100 stitches in my face. I've never had any plastic surgery. I was sewn up in the emergency room, and this is how it came out.

"Some people in this world are very beautiful, David, but I'm not one of them. I work very hard to be in the best physical shape I can be in. I make the most of my hair, makeup, and clothes. That's important to me. I want to do my best in everything.

"Negative self-images usually come from comparing oneself to others. I cannot be someone else, so I just try to be the very best Cheryl I can be. By being the best I can be, eventually I will get somewhere."

COACH ED TEMPLE DEVELOPED ATHLETES INTO OLYMPIC CHAMPIONS BY CHALLENGING THEM TO DO THEIR BEST

Coach Ed Temple was the women's track coach at Tennessee State in Nashville from 1953 to his retirement in 1993. As an undergraduate at Tennessee State, he was an accomplished sprinter, running 9.7 in the 100-yard dash and 21.5 for 220 yards. Temple was a great motivator and always challenged the young women in his program to do their best. He gave his team the name "Tigerbelles." Under Ed Temple's tutelage, the "Tigerbelles" were perennial national champions, capturing thirty-four national championships, sixteen indoors, thirteen outdoors and five in the junior meet. When budget cuts wouldn't allow him to send a team to the 1981 national championships, he determined to raise the money somehow by himself.

"I was really peeved," he admitted, "Because I had a good team. I got different organizations to sponsor us, but I still had only enough money to take four girls. That meant I had to leave some of my best athlete's home. I wanted to give the sophomores experience.

"They got out there and did their best, but I wasn't really keeping up with the points, because I thought we didn't have a chance. I didn't realize until they announced it that we had actually won the national championship with just four women. Our women had fifteen points, and the nearest team had only twelve! It was one of the highlights of my coaching career."

Coach Temple coached one of the most celebrated female athletes of all time, Wilma Rudolph. "When Wilma went to the Olympic Games in Australia in 1956, her hometown folks all thought she should win first place. I didn't expect it of her. She was too young. At age sixteen, it was a great honor and a good experience for Wilma just to be in the Olympic Games. We had six girls on that team, and she was about the fifth fastest. She came in third in the 4x4 relay race and won a bronze medal. Wilma had done her best. But she wasn't satisfied. She came home, worked hard and continued to improve on her best. On September 7, 1960, at the Olympic Games in Rome, Wilma Ruddolph became the first woman in the history of track and field to win three gold medals."

Coach Temple's Olympic champions also included Mae Faggs, Wyomia Tyus, Edith McGuire and Madeline Manning Mims, all Hall of Famers.

Ed Temple, the author of *"Run Fast, Jump High, and Only the Pure in Heart Survive,"* knows how to deal with winners, because he is a great winner himself. In 1989, already a member of four other Halls of Fame, he was inducted to the National Track and Field Hall of Fame. Temple watched his women athletes win twenty-three Olympic medals, thirteen of them gold. He was honored as the head coach of the U.S. Olympic women's team in both 1960 and 1964 and was an assistant coach in 1980, making him the only track coach to be selected three times to coach the United States Olympic Team. Ed Temple remains active in the city of Nashville.

DON THOREN BELIEVES "THE GREATEST QUALITY A COMMUNICATOR CAN HAVE IS A BELIEF IN WHAT HE IS SAYING AND A DESIRE TO HELP THE LISTENER."

One of the areas where many people fear they won't perform at their best is in standing before a large group of people and speaking. Since this is essential in so many occupations—whether it is trying to motivate a group of sales people or just making a presentation at a company meeting.

Don Thoren is the founder and president of Thoren Consulting

Group in Tempe, Arizona, a professional training company in sales, management, and personnel programs. He is also a CPAE, inductee in the National Speakers Association Speaker Hall of Fame, and past president of The National Speakers Association (NSA). I asked Don for a few tips on how people could overcome this difficulty and the fear that often goes along with public speaking.

"I believe the fear of public speaking is born out of concern for self," he replied. "The real solution to the problem is to put your concern and emphasis on the other person. If you see yourself as one who is trying to help another, you're not nearly as self-conscious. The greatest quality any communicator can have is a belief in what he is saying and a desire to help the listener. When you put those two things together, the focus is taken off yourself, and you learn to become a better communicator."

Don's extremely relaxed, poised presence on the platform gives credibility to his advice on how to do your best at presenting your thoughts to others.

JERRY HEFFEL IS INDUCTED TO THE DIRECT SELLING ASSOCIATION HALL OF FAME

It has been said that results command respect and that a person's record of performance is all the recommendation he will ever need. Having worked with Jerry Heffel for thirteen years, when it was announced in 1980 that he had become president of The Southwestern Company in Nashville, no one was surprised. He rose to the top of the oldest and one of the most respected direct sales companies in America through daily dedication to doing his best.

In addition to his responsibilities as president of Southwestern, Jerry has also served as Chairman of the Board of both the DSA (Direct Selling Association) in Washington, D.C. and the DSEF (Direct Selling Association Education Foundation). In recognition of his significant years of service and his numerous contributions to these organizations, in 1998, Jerry Heffel became the forty-third inductee to the Direct Selling Association Hall of Fame. With over thirteen million people now participating in direct sales annually, this award is quite an honor.

On May 18, 2004, at the Direct Selling Association's Annual meeting in New Orleans, Jerry was again honored with the Direct Selling Education Foundation's Circle of Honor Award. This lifetime achievement award was created by DSEF in 1988 to recognize individuals who have made extraordinary contributions to the foundation for their continuous guidance, effective leadership, vision, generosity, outstanding public service, and personal efforts and commitment.

When Jerry Heffel talks about doing your best, people listen. When I interviewed Jerry for my radio program, "The Winner's Circle," Jerry shared with the listening audience some of the following tips:

"If you'll always work hard and do more than you're asked or expected to do, then you'll always be succeeding."

"We need to take what we do very seriously, but not take ourselves too seriously."

"The hardest time to do your best is on a day-to-day basis, because it is not as exciting. That's when it really takes a tremendous amount of dedication and commitment to keep doing your best."

"The habit of reacting positively to negative circumstances is one of the most important criteria for doing your best consistently."

"Doing your best is a habit—a way of life."

Jerry Heffel continues to serve as President of The Southwestern Company. Men like Jerry have made Southwestern what it is today— a thriving direct sales company dedicated to developing character in young people.

MELVIN DAVIS WAS DEDICATED TO DOING HIS BEST IN EVERY AREA OF HIS LIFE

Having had the opportunity of sharing in the training of over 50,000 of these young people over the years, I've met some of the outstanding college students in America. One who stands out in my mind is Melvin Lee Davis, a young man dedicated to doing his best in every area of his life. Melvin came from a family of ten children in South Carolina. As one of seventeen African Americans in a student body of about 2,500 at Furman University in South Carolina, he received the Most Outstanding Freshman Award. While working his way through college, he still had time to be a student leader and served as vice-president of the student body in his junior year. He narrowly missed being elected president his senior year.

In 1972, Melvin's first summer in The Southwestern Company's program, he worked in a small city in Texas. Not owning a car didn't discourage him a bit. He carried his sales case from house to house as he walked up and down the streets. His retail business was $4,913 his first summer. Not a company record, but a solid summer.

When setting goals for his second summer, he simply said, "I'm going to do the best I can and try to increase 100 percent." He did his best and increased his retail sales to $10,963. His third summer his retail business was $14,961. His fourth, he retailed $26,709. And his fifth he retailed an impressive $33,398, earning $14,361 in commissions and finishing number six out of 6,505 salespeople company-wide. Because Melvin Davis was committed to doing his best, in time he became one of the very best.

Through the years, Melvin and I became good friends. Because of his record with Southwestern Company, he was invited to become a fulltime sales manager. He and his wife, Jackie, moved to Nashville shortly before the birth of their first child. With his good-natured, upbeat personality, Melvin made friends easily. His optimistic outlook on life made him fun to be with. He loved life so much that he caused people to enjoy it too. That's why the phone call that told of his death in a traffic accident came as such a shock.

Jackie asked me to come to South Carolina to deliver the eulogy. I was honored to be asked, yet I felt totally inadequate to put into words what a fine young man Melvin had been and how much he had meant to everyone who had known him. All I could promise was that I would do my best.

Sitting on the platform of the little country church, I looked over the crowd that had gathered to honor Melvin's memory. The wood framed building had a seating capacity of about 100, but nearly twice that many people had squeezed in. A very diverse group had assembled. Scattered among the home folks were former classmates from Furman and book people from The Southwestern Company. His best friend, Ron Hooker; his student manager, Marvin Hall; his former sales manager, Terry Weaver; and President, Jerry Heffel, were all standing in the crowded aisles.

Then they wheeled in Jackie. Her left foot, which had been injured in the accident, was bound in a cast. On her lap she held her beautiful seventeen-month-old daughter, Charsie. A slender slip of a girl, Jackie displayed a remarkable amount of courage as they parked her wheelchair to the left of the casket. Her composure had to come from the One who is the Source of real peace. As Onnie Kirk, Melvin's director of sales, was finishing his remarks, I prayed, *Lord, help me to say something that will be meaningful for Jackie.*

"My first reaction when I heard of the tragedy was to ask, 'Why'?" I began. "Why would God take someone like Melvin Davis? Such a capable young man. So dedicated. So in love with life and with so much to give."

I shared that sorrow is universal, and none of us can escape it. The world is full of pain, suffering, accidents, and despair. But the God of all comfort can be our refuge. Jesus promised, "In my Father's house are many mansions...I go to prepare a place for you." We have the assurance that Melvin has triumphed over death. He lives eternally.

Yet we miss him. God never promised we would not suffer in this life, but he has promised to give us the courage to face our sorrows. We are all saddened by loss, yet we can be thankful we had the privilege of knowing Melvin Davis. He enriched my life as he did all those who knew and loved him.

When I remember Melvin, the word commitment comes to mind. He was a committed student; a committed sales manager; a committed Christian; a committed husband and father. Many people live long lives, yet can't count on one hand the people they have influenced for good. Melvin had but a short number of years, yet he influenced more lives than most people who have lived two or three times as long. And that influence will live on.

In my eulogy I said, "Jackie, we know your loss is great. We loved him, too. Little Charsie doesn't understand what has happened and what she has lost. As she matures, she will discover that her dad was quite a man. He always did his best."

In the years since that touching experience, Melvin's memory has continued to be an inspiration to me. Not only because he always did his best, but also because he was a living example of Principle 7. This, the most important of all the principles, is the foundation upon which all the others are built.

PRINCIPLE

7

LET GOD HELP YOU

The sun was shining, and I was singing at full volume in my off-key tenor as I drove toward Nashville. My old green Chevy had finally given up the ghost. So, before leaving my sales locality, I invested in a classy looking '52 Oldsmobile to pull my U-haul full of extra books that I was taking back to headquarters. Life was sweet. I was number one! I'd made it to the top! I was about to begin my career as a district sales manager for The Southwestern Company. Oh, the thrill of victory.

Interstate 75 cut through a mountain pass, and there was Chattanooga laid out at my feet. The magnificent view seemed symbolic of the world stretched out before me. Even though my total commissions of $9,300 for the summer wouldn't be quite enough to pay my entire debt, it had put a good-sized dent in it, and, boy, did my future look bright. Ah, yes, life was great.

Thump, thump, thump. At first I tried to ignore the noise that was coming from under the back end of the car, but as the vibrations got rougher, I pulled onto the shoulder. I walked all around the Olds, kicking at the tires, but there was no flat. I started off again, but the thump, thump persisted. I decided I'd better not take any chances and pulled into a service station. The mechanic unhooked the trailer and put the car up on the rack.

"How far do you have to go?" he asked. "Nashville."

"That's all?"

"Yeah."

"No problem. You'll make it."

"You're sure about that?"

"Yes, sir, I'm sure."

So we hooked the trailer back up and off I went. About two or three miles further on down the road, I braked to slow down on a hill and realized I had no brakes! Fortunately, I hadn't been going too fast, and I was able to pull off and on the shoulder of the road several times until the car finally slowed to a stop.

I sat there a minute, giving my heart time to calm back down. Suddenly a man came running up, yelling at the top of his voice, "Get out of your car! Quick! There are flames shooting five feet out the back! Move, now!"

As I jumped out, I spotted the flames coming from under the car, blazing all around my gas tank. *"This baby is fixing to explode!"* I thought.

"Unhook your trailer! Get your stuff out of the car! Move!" the man ordered as he proceeded to unhook the trailer. "I'm an ex-police officer—I know what I'm doing. Now, hurry up!"

I started grabbing my clothes and throwing them. Every time I put my head inside that car to grab more things, I thought the car would blow. The ex-officer assured me that cars explode only in the movies and on TV, but I didn't feel very secure about it. I managed to get most of my clothes out of the car while he disengaged the trailer. Within three minutes my car was totally engulfed in flames.

Then, I remembered the $600 in checks I had left in the glove compartment. I'd paid only $300 for the car, but the checks brought my loss up to about $900. I just stood there and watched it all go up in flames. The traffic was stopped as far back as I could see. People got out of their cars and milled around, watching that baby burn. The horn was blowing in a dying protest at its untimely end.

It was an interesting contrast. A half hour before, I'd been on top of the world. Now, I was watching my transportation turn to ashes amidst the commotion of all the people walking around. One lady came running up and stood right next to me. "It's burning! It's burning!" she wailed. "Whose car is that?"

"Mine."

"Yours! That car is yours? It's going to burn!"

"Ma'am, thank you very much, but it is already burning. As a matter of fact, if you will look closely, you will see it has already burned." She was so overly concerned that I had to laugh a bit at her agitation.

"Oh, my! What are you going to do?"

"That's a very good question. I'm not sure. I'm just thankful I wasn't in the car. Thankful we got the trailer unhooked."

"How can you be so calm?"

"Well, Ma'am," I said smiling at her, "It's a long story, but I've learned to accept my situation exactly as it is..."

She looked at me as if I had a screw loose, but for me everything was falling into place. My principles worked here, too! It suddenly dawned on me that the 7 Principles that had helped me turn my life around weren't just for selling—or for managing. They were principles for living that could be applied to any situation or profession. That revelation meant more to me than the loss of the car or the inconvenience of having to hire someone to haul me and my trailer the rest of the way to Nashville. I'd learned 7 Principles for successful living!

I was filled with a tremendous sense of gratitude, for it was surely the seventh principle, "Let God Help You," that had made it possible for me to bounce back. Just a few months before, my confidence had been at an all-time low. I had little hope of recovering financially and a lot of fear about the future. Yet God had helped me to accept my situation the way it was. Then He'd given me the courage to be willing to fail. He had helped me discipline myself to make daily preparations on a consistent basis. He'd given me the strength to work professionally to pace myself to do whatever needed to be done. Through his grace I had been able to live in the present and take it one day at a time throughout the summer. Most of all, God had enabled me to do my best.

Early into the summer while I was driving to Nashville, I had prayed "Lord, you know I believe in you, although I don't always show it. Thank you for being faithful even during my times of unfaithfulness. Forgive me for my inconsistencies."

"I don't know how I'm going to get through this summer, but it says in Philippians 4:13 that I can do all things through Christ who strengthens me, and I choose to believe that. Please give me the strength to work hard, stay on schedule, and do my best, regardless of what I sell. I believe you will."

And He did. And He'll help you too, *if you'll let Him.*

Does this mean that the six previous principles are invalid without faith in God? No, definitely not! But I found that for me personally the chances of being able to apply the principles consistently are much greater with God's help.

COACH SAID TO ME, "...THERE IS NOTHING MORE EXCITNG THAN A PERSONAL RELATIONSHIP WITH JESUS CHRIST."

Coach Bob Davenport has been one of the greatest influences in my life. All through college he was a living example of what God can do in a life. I'll never forget the day he said to me, "David, I know it seems to you as if my All-American honors and professional football experiences would have been exciting. They were okay, but fleeting. I can honestly tell you that there is nothing more exciting than a personal relationship with Jesus Christ."

Coach Davenport went on to explain that during his freshman year at UCLA he had taken a course sponsored by the newly organized Campus Crusade for Christ: "It was a rather unique, but not overly religious group, and it afforded me the opportunity of seriously investigating the possibility of Christ being what he claimed to be—the Son of God. After completing UCLA, I realized that of all the courses I'd taken in earning my degree, that noncredit course taught by Dr. Bill Bright, the founder of Campus Crusade for Christ, had been the most important, significant, and life-changing of all."

COLONEL JIM IRWIN THOUGHT, "HOW BIG AM I?"

Over the years, I've had this same truth reemphasized by many others. One of the most inspiring testimonies was that of Colonel Jim Irwin when he shared his experiences about his trip to the moon. "When I looked out and saw the earth only as big as a little marble, I thought, "How big am I? I'm just a speck of dust—if that big—compared to the universe. Yet this little speck has the capacity to know God! To know the One who holds the universe. To know His love, and have His direction. For the first time I saw—felt—God's love for the earth, and John 3:16 took on a special significance: For God so loved the world that he gave his one and only son that whosoever believes in him shall not perish, but have eternal life. I realized then that God loved that little blue marble. That little planet. He loved all the billions of people on it. And he loved me!

"I realized that my relationship with Jesus Christ was the most precious thing I had, and I renewed that relationship on my journey to the moon."

"I DECIDED MY THEME SONG
WAS GOING TO BE "I DID IT MY WAY."

It isn't necessary to take a trip to the moon to come to the same conclusion Colonel Irwin did. Shortly after Don Thoren had been elected president of the National Speakers Association, he shared with me: "My life tends not to have traumatic turning points, but evolution. When I started out in business, I decided my theme song was going to be 'I Did It My Way.' I looked on Christians as a bunch of cripples who had to blame their failure or success on someone other than themselves.

"Then in a slow but steady way, I found myself coming closer to the Lord. Picking up a Bible in a hotel room and reading from it occasionally, going to church once in a while, and talking with a fraternity brother from college, I finally came to realize that I could not earn a relationship with the Lord. I could only accept it. In a hotel room in Minneapolis, Minnesota, I told the Lord that I wanted to accept his gift of salvation, and was turning my life over to him.

"There was no ringing of bells, but there was a great transition in my life. I was no longer afraid. I quit worrying about myself and whether I would be a success. He gave me serenity."

"AT AGE SEVENTY-NINE, I HAD
ACCOMPLISHED A GREAT DEAL IN BUSINESS,"
COLONEL SANDERS TOLD ME.

While it is a great advantage to begin your relationship with God at an early age, it is not necessarily a prerequisite to success. Colonel Sanders had experienced a great deal of success before he "took God" as his partner. "At age seventy-nine, I had accomplished a great deal in business," the Colonel told me, "yet I still sensed a void. Something was not quite right. Then I attended a revival service in a church that was not even of my faith. Since the decision I made that night, I have had an assurance God's going to take care of me."

NOW IS YOUR TIME TO WIN

DEAN JONES WAS MAKING $15,000 A WEEK, "BUT THERE WAS AN EMPTINESS I WAS CONSTANTLY TRYING TO FILL."

Even though veteran Hollywood actor, Dean Jones was making $15,000 a week, he told me, he was once so depressed that he stood at a motel window one night and thought, *"If something doesn't happen in my life, I'm gonna blow the top of my head off."*

"What caused such dissatisfaction with life?" I asked him.

"I don't really know, David, but there was an emptiness I was constantly trying to fill. The more success and money I had, the more miserable I seemed to become. Anyone who wants to make it in show business feels that success will satisfy him, but it doesn't. Money and fame can be nice, but they simply do not satisfy. I have since found that God is the only true source of fulfillment and satisfaction."

"HEY, GOD, I BELIEVE YOU ARE TRYING TO TELL ME SOMETHING."

Dean Jones just contemplated suicide, but Nashville songwriter, Marijohn Wilkin, actually attempted it. "I don't know much about guns," she confided, "but one Easter morning I was so despondent I put a bullet in a gun, a long gun, not a handgun. I leaned over the barrel and pushed the trigger, and the bullet did the craziest thing. It deflected under my chin and landed on the floor. I tried it again and exactly the same thing happened. I looked up and said, 'Hey, God, I believe you are trying to tell me something.'

"Then I thought I had to figure why God had kept me from dying. My depression stopped, and I became more aware of everything around me. I started reading something besides Billboard and Mickey Spillane murder mysteries. I did hours and hours of study, going through various religions in search of something to fulfill my needs. Then songs like 'One Day at a Time' started pouring out, and I truly 'Returned to the God of my Childhood.'"

"GOD, IF YOU'RE REAL, LET ME KNOW."

It isn't necessary to become desperate before turning to God for help. Four-time Gold Medal winner, John Naber, was still in high school when he heard a speaker who made him stop and consider the direc-

102

tion his life was going. "I was never a boozer or a drug addict," he recalls, "but I sensed a need in my life. One night in the privacy of my own bedroom, I prayed, *'God, if you're real, let me know'*. The immediate response after that was an assurance that he was there. It's my faith in his presence and sovereignty over my life that enables me to handle adversity as well as success. God promises some things. He loves me. I don't have to earn his love. He put sports and everything else into proper perspective and allows us to get the most out of life."

CHARLIE JONES REALIZED, "I WAS YOUNG, HEALTHY, HAD A FINE WIFE, AND A GREAT FUTURE, BUT I KNEW FROM THE SCRIPTURES THAT I ALSO HAD A GREAT NEED."

"A young friend introduced me to the Bible when I was twenty-two," Charlie "Tremendous" Jones told me. "He left me alone. I read John 1:12, 3:16, and 5:24, and I accepted Christ. I was young, healthy, had a fine wife, and a great future, but I knew from the Scriptures that I also had a great need. A motivator could have reached my head with that thought, but it took the Bible to reach my heart.

"I talk to businessmen all the time who think they don't need God. I just tell them, 'That's wonderful. Hang in there as long as you can, and do all you can to keep away from God. You don't need God to be happy and make money. I got all I needed without God.'

"But the fellow without God knows in his heart that he's a dead man. He knows he's got a happy act—nothing more. The time will come when he realizes he can't go on in his own strength, and then he'll find it easy and wonderful to receive Christ as Savior."

"HE NEVER FORCED PEOPLE TO DECIDE. BUT WHEN WE REALIZE THAT WE NEED HIM AND WANT HIM TO FORGIVE THE MESS WE'VE MADE OF OUR LIVES, THEN HE WILL."

Former Miss America, Cheryl Salem tells of accepting Christ when she was fourteen. "I made this quiet decision to accept him—a quality decision. A lot of people grow up in church, and they know that Jesus loves them and that he died for all the world, but they've never realized that he's done it for them. If I were the only person on the earth, he would have done it for me.

"Jesus wasn't a pushy person. He never screamed and yelled and made people follow him. He led a quiet life, and if they followed him, they followed him. He never forced people to decide. But when we realize that we need him and want him to forgive the mess we've made of our lives, then he will. It's that simple."

"WHEN I DISCOVERED THAT, I MADE A COMMITMENT, AND HE FILLED THE VACUUM IN MY LIFE," COACH TOM LANDRY SAID.

"I'd heard about Jesus all my life, but I didn't really know who he was until I was 34," Coach Tom Landry said. "I'd accomplished everything I'd set out to do in sports, yet there was a void in my life. I was going to quit football because I'd done everything in coaching I could do. I had a restlessness and emptiness before I discovered Christ.

"I began attending a Bible study group. I thought I knew all the Bible I needed. I knew the Easter story and the Christmas story, but I didn't even know the gospel of Jesus Christ—that he had died for me. When I discovered that, I made a commitment, and he filled the vacuum in my life.

"Now I realize that a person without Christ is handicapped. God made us in his image, and he made us unique. Therefore, we're going to find fulfillment in life only through a right relationship with God through Jesus Christ. Once we do that, we won't worry as much, and we'll have the capability of coming closer to reaching our God-given potential. Anyone who hasn't made that discovery is handicapped even if he doesn't realize it."

AS COACH WOODEN WAS TALKING, HE SLOWLY PULLED A LITTLE CROSS OUT OF HIS POCKET AND PLACED IT IN MY HAND.

"I was always known as one who attended church," Coach John Wooden told me. "However, it was mostly for appearances' sake, until I accepted Christ in my late thirties. I've found that a committed Christian can accept adversity and failure better than someone who is not committed to Christ."

As he was talking, he slowly pulled a little cross out of his pocket and placed it in my hand. "When I entered the service in 1943,"

Coach Wooden explained, "my minister gave me this little cross that he hoped would help me in times of tension. I've carried this cross with me ever since. It's a simple reminder of the fact that I'm a Christian. It isn't magic and it isn't meant to protect me from every physical harm; it's just a reminder. Whenever I'm under any sort of emotional pressure, it gives me a better realization of the someone who is in control. It reminds me of the life-changing decision I made years ago."

Looking at the cross in my hand reminded me of another destiny-changing decision made upon a rocky hill outside Jerusalem long ago. Three men were being executed in a cold, heartless manner that day while the uncompassionate, bloodthirsty mob jeered. A sign had been posted upon the center cross with a message written in three languages: THIS IS THE KING OF THE JEWS.

One of the victims, his face distorted as much by hate as by fear and pain, joined the mocking crowd in scoffing at the Man on the center cross. "So, you're the Messiah, are you? Prove it by saving yourself—and us, too, while you're at it!"

There was no reply from the battered form in the center of the scene, but strangely, the third man rose to his defense. "Don't you even fear God when you're dying?" he demanded of the mocker. "We deserve to die for our evil deeds, but this man hasn't done one thing wrong." Accepting his situation—hopeless though it seemed—he turned to the gentle-faced Man, who had been so cruelly disfigured. "Jesus, remember me when you come into your Kingdom."

With tender eyes, Jesus looked at the dying thief and promised, "Today you will be with me in Paradise."

The conversation lasted only *thirty seconds,* but a destiny was changed forever.

TO THE READER

So, how can you get the most from this gold mine you hold in your hand? Go back and review each chapter. You might want to devote a week or more to the first one, seeking the best method for you to work that particular principle into your own life. Then, go on to the second...and the third. In two months or less, you might not recognize yourself and your accomplishments as your income and your desire to excel increase.

Og Mandino

David Dean can be contacted at the following address:

David Dean and Associates, Inc.
8485 E. McDonald Dr. #284
Scottsdale, AZ 85250-4920
Email: DavidDean@DavidDeanandAssociates.com
www.DavidDeanandAssociates.com